BARNYARD
TO
BOARDROOM:
BUSINESS BASICS

by Don Aslett

Barnyard to Boardroom: Business Basics. Copyright © 2008 by Don Aslett, a revised and expanded edition of the book titled **Everything I Needed to Know About Business I Learned in the Barnyard**, copyright © 1993 by Don A. Aslett. Illustrations copyright © 2006 Don Aslett. Printed and bound in the United States of America. All rights reserved. No part of this book may be reproduced in any form or by any electronic or mechanical means including information storage and retrieval systems without permission in writing from the publisher, except by a reviewer, who may quote brief passages in a review.

Published by

Marsh Creek Press
PO Box 700
Pocatello, Idaho 83204
Phone 208-232-3535
Fax 208-235-5481
www.aslett.com

ISBN 13 978-0-937750-36-0
ISBN 10 0-937750-36-0

To purchase this book in quantity at a discount, contact the publisher above.

Illustrators: Craig LaGory, Robert Betty

Editor: Carol Cartaino

Production Manager: Tobi Alexander

Graphic Design: Ryan Roghaar

Contributor: Shane Campbell,
            Varsity University Manager

This, my twentieth book, is dedicated to my Father.

Duane Aslett
1909–1983

A totally moral man, kind to animals, to the land, and to all his family. Just being around him, anytime, was more than a college education. As to his management and productivity, I've yet to meet an equal—he was brilliant!

Other business books
by Don Aslett

Done!
(How to Accomplish Twice as Much
in Half the Time—at Home and at the Office)

The Office Clutter Cure

How to Be #1 with Your Boss

Keeping Work Simple (with Carol Cartaino)

Cleaning Up for a Living (with Mark Browning)

How I Swept My Way to the Top: The Don Aslett Story

Speak Up!
(A Step-by-Step Guide for Presenting Powerful Public Speeches)

Acknowledgments

There is a time and place for all of us "big businesspeople" (executives, professionals, and power players), well-schooled, well-tailored, and well-positioned, to sit back and have some plain rural folks teach us some real down-to-earth ethics and master management moves.

I am deeply thankful for the advice and inspiration of all those men and women manning the barnyard, like my parents and grandparents, the hired hands, the seasonal helpers, and the plain old farmers everywhere, especially in Idaho and Ohio and some of you corn farmers in Kansas, too!

Some of my farm heroes include:
Duane & Opal Aslett – Leon Aslett
Hoot & Ross Gibson – Ron Hawks
Monte Sorenson – "Toots" Nelson
Floyd Kisling – Oscar Stimson
Jim Burgoyne – Gerald Doughty
Lynn Bullock – Estelle Ricketts
Art Kelly – Ezra Taft & Valdo Benson
Bobby Erickson – Bill Johnson
Walter Bowman – Andrew Ross
John McNabb – Carter Luther
Virgil Likely – John Felthusen
Dean Palmer – Tim Beeler
Jim & Martha Chambers
Mike Scotch

P.S. Let's not forget those animals, either. The animals of the field, forest, and barnyard have contributed a lot to communication over the centuries. Our goose would be cooked without them. We'd be counting our chickens before they hatched, changing horses in the middle of streams, acting piggish or stubborn as a mule, giving people bum steers, and waiting around until the cows come home. If we took the animals out of our alphabet, world literature would be poor as a church mouse. Animals have made our pages—and our stages—crow, strut, leap, and hop; helped remind us that instinct is as important as intelligence. Chickened out, bull-headed, early bird, greener pastures, calf eyes, sly as a fox, and ahhh, even a roll in the hay—all of these and thousands more of our everyday expressions came from animals and the barnyard. They should have received the Pulitzer Prize of the Pasture, so here, not looking a gift horse in the mouth, is a wholehearted tribute to them. (How many of your own life's best principles, clearest messages, and surest inspirations also came from animals?)

Table of Contents

Acknowledgments .... page vi
Introduction .... page 1

North Forty .... page 6
Lessons from the chickens
It only takes smart dogs once
Pedigree is no guarantee
Lead ropes and leadership
Not all bulls breed
Animals in heat do dumb things ...**AND MANY MORE**

South Forty .... page 48
Down wind is a bad place to be
If you feed the stock, they stay in the corral
Steers try
"Root, hog, or die!"
Know where your pitchforks are
Spurs make a good horse buck ...**AND MANY MORE**

East Forty .... page 92
Keep your harness out of the rain
The more mane, the more burrs
Empty corrals still cost
When you overfeed, you waste
You can't horse around with authority
The toughest discipline ...**AND MANY MORE**

West Forty .... page 130
Barnyard consultants
Dumb animals? Don't you believe it!
It isn't the breed, it's the individual
There's always a crowd in the shade
Horns look bad, but it's the hooves you have to watch
Read before you feed! ...**AND MANY MORE**

Appendix: Teacher's Guide .... page 165

Introduction

Managerial prerogative... Management matrix... Synergy... Total asset turnover... Strategic positioning... Progressive management... Marketing analysis... Qualitative assessment... Statistical basis... Operating profits... Investment management... Linear regression... Liquidity ratios... Leaseholder improvements... Data analysis techniques... Cost/time analysis... High performance team... Creative problem-solving... Group consensus decisions... Win-win deals... Innovative development... Value engineering methodology... Quality circles... Project management... Employee development... Situational appraisal... Decision analysis... Payback analysis... Break-even analysis... Consolidated statement of income... Current maturities... Communication links... Venture marketing... Par growth rate... Peer management... Response-oriented departments... Database directive... Job enhancement... Excellence-oriented management... Incremental innovation...

I'm with the bull on the right—business just isn't that complicated. In fact I'd be willing to bet the best businesspeople in the world today are those who know and use the basics. All the executive-itis fluff that's been infused into business has accomplished only one thing, and that is to provide jobs for a lot of professional analysts, advisors, counselors, and promoters. Good old business itself is so basic, so simple, so much fun—but add all that manipulative manure to a simple office, shop, store, or studio, and it becomes a mass of bluffing, butt-covering, posturing, and politics.

I remember a hunting trip into the Idaho Primitive Area that several of my managers and I took with our sons. On the way there one of the sons, a freshman in college, was studying for a final.

"What is the test on?" I asked.

"Business 101," he answered, patting a fat textbook respectfully.

"Mind if I look at your book?" Although I founded and ran a highly successful cleaning company (now a multimillion-dollar operation) and a half-dozen other businesses, and had written many bestselling books, I was largely self-taught. I was curious to see what the formal teachings were on all the subjects I learned the hard way. As I flipped the pages, I became intrigued with the complexity of it. A beginner's book? Stopping at "Inventory" and reading a bit, I thought up to now that I knew what inventory was, having run a profitable mailorder house, and handled all types of stock and inventory in my cleaning business for 50 years. But in this book, I couldn't understand it. I flipped to Payroll/Deductions and read—it was all Greek to me. I'd run payroll myself by hand for years, and now have four full-time employees in my payroll department, yet I couldn't figure out what this book was saying. It was the most forbidding, complicated exploration I'd ever seen. With a couple of charts from the IRS, the Labor Department, and the state, and about 15 minutes of instruction, a 12-year-old could do payroll. Yet here, riding along on a hunting trip, a 50-year-old, well-seasoned businessman (veteran of not one but several businesses, chairman of the board and millionaire to boot) couldn't fathom this freshman business book.

"Do you understand all this, Eric?" I asked.

"It's tough," he said.

"Tough? I've never seen the simple elements of business made so complex. Maybe I've lost it since college, but I can't even understand what it says."

"I paid sixty-eight dollars for this book," he added.

I paged through more of the basic business functions—Taxes, Licenses, and Overhead. I was sure I'd never even pass the test. Then I began reading aloud to the other four executives and a brilliant CEO, and they roared with laughter and groaned at how incredibly sophisticated the simple secrets of running a good, profitable operation had been made here. We were actually doing these things every day, but we'd never manage it if we attempted to follow such intricate structures and procedures. When I thought about it, it really upset me,

Barnyard to Boardroom

charging a sharp kid $68 (plus all that tuition) to expose him to such a snarled synopsis of what could be a great career and profession.

If that kid had one ounce of logic or common sense, it would soon be permanently muddled. I decided right then that one of these days I would write a better book on business, one so simple that anyone could understand it, whether they were running their first lemonade stand on the corner, or going for their MBA. I'd tell them how to DO business instead of talk and play business.

As I was casting about for a format, one day I heard the famous words "horse sense" and that was it. Most of my business and life savvy, I suddenly realized, in fact comes from the farm—the barnyard. Every principle of business I actually use could be traced back to a lesson learned back at the ol' corral. For sure I didn't learn much business from my own years in college, which included even way back then a lot of hot air and outdated information in what business courses I did have. Everything that really works, I learned from my early practical experience back home on the range.

Horse sense and the habit of 16-hour workdays is what I left the farm for college with, no formal business training, but the conviction instilled by my parents that earning and paying your own way is the most exciting and honorable way to live. As I sought a sound, secure way to defray my future college costs, the head of the university placement office said he was flooded with requests for someone to do not only lawn and garden work and general maintenance, but *cleaning*. So I put an ad in the paper, and learned by good old hands-on experience how to clean windows and carpets and just about everything else in a home or commercial building. I hired one fellow student, then three, then twenty, and later fifty and then a hundred. Since that modest beginning back in the 50's, I've hired tens of thousands of people to work in and run my businesses.

With only a barnyard business background, I built that college expediency into a three-state operation by the time I graduated. By then I realized that I knew more about cleaning toilets than I did about dissecting frogs, so I stayed in the profession and built my little company into one of the top in the industry. For every problem and circumstance that popped up along the way, it seemed I always found a solution in my childhood dealings with pigs, cows, and chickens. Impressed by the farm recordkeeping I learned in FFA (Future Farmers of America), and by the inscriptions my father and grandfather made with stubby pencils on barn doors, I kept a journal of my experiences and impressions and how I did things.

And now here, in the following pages, I'll pass on what the pigs and the pasture passed on to me during those wonderful early days of pure education. The secrets, the real basics, of business.

What's so fascinating about a barnyard?

If you don't know, you're in for a great treat. The barnyard, usually located North or South of the house (those East and West winds carry odor, you know) is the Pentagon of production, the heart of the farm body, the Wall Street of livestock, the Madison Avenue of manure, the headquarters, the home office, of the whole farm. You arrive there daily, earliest of anyplace on the farm, and end up there latest. It's your warehouse and headquarters, the place where your stock advances and declines (is born and dies), and where not only yours, but everyone's food comes from—meat, milk, cheese, eggs, butter, corn, wheat, carrots and potatoes. As well as leather and wool and raw materials for much of what we wear and use.

As you drive past them most barnyards may look scenic and inactive, but I assure you there is more going on in a two-story barn and its adjoining fields and pens, than in a thirty-story office building. Amidst the oink-oinks here and the oink-oinks there, is a lot of intelligence.

The average land around a barnyard when I was growing up was 160 acres, and those four, forty-acre sections—the North Forty, South Forty, East Forty, and West Forty—each had a good solid semester's worth of education to offer.

Here it is, straight from the horse's mouth.

North Forty

Lessons from the chickens

It's unfair to these industrious, clean-cut birds that they've been reduced to profitmakers for Colonel Sanders, and their name is synonymous with "coward." (As in "you big chicken," or "chicken hearted.") Some of the best lessons of life and business can be learned from them.

Lesson 1:
Helping at the wrong time weakens and kills.

Eggs are laid and left under the hen, or put in an incubator. Then we can't wait for them to hatch! When the time comes and the egg moves and cheeps and starts opening, we always want to help that little baby chick struggling to get out. DON'T. If you start cracking the egg and peeling the shell off, the baby bird inside will wither and die. Its survival depends on pecking its own way out.

How many employees or subordinates have we "let out" or smoothed the way, prepared the path for, only to have them wither and fail in the end? People, like chicks, become fit and strong making their own way. Letting someone struggle to emerge and develop is wisdom; stealing their struggle only stifles them.

Lesson 2:
Make them scratch.

When we were old enough to do chores back on the ranch, one of the first jobs we got was feeding the chickens. Our flock was served half a honey bucket full of wheat kernels. My attempt to pour it all into a pile was thwarted by my mother, who put her hand in the bucket and then threw the grains all over the place as the chickens ran enthusiastically to hunt and dig for them.

"Chickens need to scratch for exercise, so toss the food all over. When you pile it up, or put it in a feeder, they just stand and eat and fight each other." That taught me clearly that the easy way wasn't the best. I'd rather scratch and dig and even go hungry before accepting government handouts or subsidies, for instance. (I've been a mighty thin chicken a few times, too.)

Lesson 3:
How to keep 'em laying.

When I was ten the whole chicken flock came under my care, all eighteen of them. My instructions were to feed them regularly, exact amounts, no skipping or guessing. I was getting eighteen eggs daily—100 percent return. If I missed a day or mis-measured their rations, forgot the water or didn't keep the coop clean, egg production fell off. They responded to consistency like magic. We used five dozen eggs a week ourselves, and I got to sell the other five dozen for twenty cents a dozen. Every week a silver dollar went into an old cheese box, and I learned well to equate success with care. It's worked this way in every business venture I've ever been involved in.

Years later, if a crew wasn't producing what they were capable of accomplishing, I needed to look to see if the coop was clean (did they have good leadership, clear instructions and expectations?). Were food and water (the necessary tools and supplies, decent pay, and raises when called for) being provided in a timely manner?

Lesson 4:
It's not the cost of the chicken, it's the cost of the feed.

Someone asked me not long ago, "How much does a chicken cost?" and the short answer is less than a dollar, if you buy it young, two or three bucks for most chickens, and maybe as much as five dollars for that fancy breed you fell in love with at the county fair. But the true cost of a chicken is all the corn and laying mash and grit, etc., it eats in a lifetime, plus the fresh bedding it needs to keep it clean, the space in your chicken house you have to allow for it, the chicken wire you need to keep it safe, and the antibiotics you have to buy when it comes down with any of the 10,000 chicken ailments. If you added it all up, the cost of one little feathered friend is pretty impressive. Think about that before you buy another chicken, add another vehicle to your fleet, load up on low-volume inventory, or hire a new employee you don't really need.

Lesson 5:
Chest beating is only noise.

Competitors and ambitious employees in the business world do this well—oversell themselves. They're forever beating their statistical or literal chest. If you take it seriously, you'll lose not only profits and perspective, but your composure.

A strutting rooster is our instructor here. I remember well walking into the barnyard when I was only five or six years old. After sizing me up a big old rooster charged me—leaped on my chest, squawking and beating his wings and pecking away. It was pure terror, between the noise and his beak tapping my shirt and belt. Then Mother appeared, and the rooster, recognizing her as the person who swings the axe, released me and ran off.

I was a quivering mass of jelly after that attack. Mother walked me to the house, washed my feather-beaten face, and explained that the rooster was only bluffing. His wings couldn't hurt you, and his beak or claws couldn't either (as long as you kept your eyes shielded) through several layers of clothes. All that noise and commotion was only to scare you out of his pen (office or affairs).

Later Dad came in, and when Mother informed him the rooster had "Flogged me unmercifully," Dad said, "Remember, flogging roosters have their necks stuck out, and a stuck-out neck is easy to wring." I believed my parents, but avoided rooster territory after that until the day my uncle taught me to wring chicken necks (that, by the way, was the fate of the next flogger!).

Those in business who crow and flap their wings to terrorize others will suffer many neck wringings during their business life.

Lesson 6:
First roosters and second roosters.

In the chicken kingdom there is, among the male chauvinist chickens, the first rooster and the second rooster. The first rooster is generally the biggest, wisest, most elegant and beautiful rooster of all. The second rooster has only a kind of vice-president, assistant manager status. The irony of this, as in business leadership, is that the first rooster, because of his position, has to spend almost all his time fighting, protecting and enlarging his domain, supervising it and defending it from encroachment. This leaves little or no time for eating or romance, not to mention dodging that Sunday dinner plate (they come for the biggest and best, you know). The second rooster, because he's not nearly as visible as his superior, is rarely threatened, and he gets plenty of food, rest, and hens for himself, while the first rooster is busy fighting everything to preserve his position.

I found out quickly in business that the second rooster position was a safe one, and once they reach it many are happy to occupy it until retirement. They're never to blame, yet have a respected name, while the head man of the organization has the constant burden of responsibilities of all kinds, the constant threat of the axe, and little time for fun or feasting.

I observed all this in the chicken kingdom for years before I saw it repeated in the boardroom. But the position of head rooster, despite the drawbacks, is still the most exciting. And the wise old rooster ultimately outlives them all, because he runs lean and mean. The second rooster doesn't have much to do but get horny and hungry, so he gets fat and flabby and sooner or later butchered. The first rooster wins the loyalty of stockholders, too, because he spends his time watching the flock instead of exploiting them.

Lesson 7:
Don't put all your eggs in one basket.

You really believe this old farm saying the first time you drop the basket, and come to appreciate the principle in business we call "diversifying." Having three or four different crops instead of one big single crop offers some security—if one or two crops freeze, are attacked by disease or insects, or turn out to have no market, you have two others to bring you through. A handyman handy at only one thing will be in trouble if his one well-honed skill is not requested or goes out of style. Specialization may have its advantages or even be necessary in some services (like medicine); however the general businessperson, store, or contractor is much more "hireable" if he or she has more merchandise or skills to offer and doesn't depend fully on a single source, or one big harvest. Why just clean walls when without much more investment you can clean ceilings? There is efficiency in one basket, but not security.

Lesson 8:
With assets one mistake is too many.

Attempting twenty years later to teach my own children my chicken lessons in life, my wife and I bought fifty baby chicks. We managed, with the aid of a brooder and careful penning, to raise them to the point that they'd become pullets, or teenager chickens. We also owned a Brittany Spaniel, born and bred to find and deliver feathered fowl. Just one single day out of a hundred we left the chickens out unattended. Late that afternoon our dog showed up with guilty feathers on his lip, after killing every single chicken.

Even your best assets are only safe when you have them 100 percent in control.

Lesson 9:
Roost high!
(You can figure that one out yourself.)

Use thick gloves when you handle barbed wire

Whether we like it or not, sometimes we have to deal with it, and in business or on the farm, barbed wire can cut you bad. Since at least 75 percent of any stretch of barbed wire is actually smooth and harmless, however, we're always tempted to tough it out. We'll just grab it or try to climb over it anyway, just "carefully." But those little points are sharp and strong, and you can't be careful enough to escape them entirely. And when they get you those barbs will make you bleed.

So always arm for the barb (in contracts, too, which may mean you need a thick padding of the right kind of words at all the danger points).

Save all surprises for birthday parties!

One of the very first principles I learned in the barnyard was that animals don't like surprises of any kind, good or bad. So when you entered the barnyard you did so whistling, singing, or banging the milk bucket a little, to let the animals know it was you and not a coyote, cougar, or cow ghost, or something.

Surprising animals will result in some real disasters. When we were kids, jumping up from behind a haystack used to be great sport, to see the cows almost leap out of their hides and race, glassy-eyed, to a big milling group at the other side of the corral. Sometimes they'd jerk their head back out of the manger so fast they'd snap a board somewhere and that would really set them off. Ask a horseman with a broken nose how he got it. Most likely from scaring or surprising a horse while its head was down eating, drinking, or resting and it yanked up suddenly and smacked him right in the old snoot. A horse head and neck can move at a speed that surpasses a Tyson punch. We barnyard veterans can also testify to the reward for creeping up behind an animal and saying "boo." You'll get a real kick out of it, I assure you.

Me and most other bosses in business also hate surprises, good or bad. When something is up, or went wrong, I want to know about it now, not have it announced to me at a party or at payroll time, or held from the night before until morning. Too many wait till the end of the month or the year or the end of a relationship to find out. Whether it's a good or bad announcement, you won't be prepared for it, and awkwardness and inefficiency will always be the result.

It only takes smart dogs once

I saw the results of a porcupine many times before I ever saw a porcupine. One of our dogs would come up to us whining and shaking his head, and through a pincushion spread of porcupine quills, his pained eyes would look up and beg us to help. I held the squirming dog as Dad yanked the deeply penetrated, oversize needle looking things out with a pair of pliers. It was ghastly to watch and surely no fun to experience either. Those quills were in the dog's lips, nose, cheeks, and even inside his mouth, in his tongue. As Dad pulled the last few out, he said, "Well, if he's a smart dog he won't stick his nose in the same place again." That dog didn't, but our next dog did. So since Dad was gone at the moment I had to de-quill the howling hound, and I wisely told my little brother who was holding the dog, "Well, if he's a smart dog he won't stick his nose in the same place again." However this dog wasn't that smart and did it again, and again. The first time we had pity on him for a hard-learned lesson, the next time, a little pity, but we did call the dog "Stupid." The third time we were irritated (it took lots of time and strength to get the quills out)—we did help him, but kind of acknowledged he got what he deserved, if he was dumb enough to keep going back to get stuck again and again.

We had a neighbor, likewise, who the first time patiently and lovingly pulled a great mass of quills out of his big black hound's face and mouth, and the very next day the dog came back again with another faceful. This time there was a fearful struggle between master and mongrel to remove them. The following day the dog showed up with yet another snoutful of those ugly little arrows, and the minute it was de-quilled, it was off to the dog pound.

We all take the risk of the sniffing dog as we explore business leads and opportunities, and how often we, too, get stuck… with a bad account, a bad product, or a bad report. And then we, too, have to go and have our wounds restored. Once, we can say shame on them (that did it), however if we get taken twice or more exactly the same way, it's "shame on me." I see managers in my own business get stuck, then restored and forgiven and reinstated. Then in full knowledge they go right back and get another faceful of stickers from the same source. This time, as with the dog, few of us really feel full pity, but we will help. Then they repeat the act again and most of us feel the same as we did for the repeating dog: *You got what you deserved.*

A good moral for us as well as for our four-footed friends... *keep away from the people or situations that stick you—forgive but don't forget.*

You'll eventually answer for anything (junk!) you leave lying around

After fixing or changing, opening or building something in the barnyard, tossing down the old part or the packaging and just leaving it there is so easy. So some sloppy farmers and some green kids, like me and my brothers, would toss pieces of harness, ends and bits of boards, snips of wire, almost-empty containers or lids on the ground in the corral, yard or barn. Within days the animal droppings and the straw would swallow them up. But they always reappeared.

"Bang! Psssst!..." One of the big tires on the tractor would go, and Dad would pull out a harrow spike. Or right in the middle of our best hay-hauling record—click, clink, clickety clank—four inches of cast-off harness chain would catch in the power takeoff of the tractor and twist it. Or a cow would limp in with a piece of gate latch in its hoof, or a bolt would shear on the loader, from some wire hidden under the manure.

Any junk—empty sacks, old nails, or broken tools—left around would eventually cause an accident. Someone would stumble over it, or it would injure or choke an animal. Untucked-in shirts got caught in augers or power takeoffs and took fingers, arms, or a life; unclean facilities caused fires or cave-ins; carelessly tossed twine or baling wire damaged equipment and delayed jobs, or caused arguments.

Carelessly discarded junk is always a problem. You pay the price a hundred-fold in time and repairs. This is a good lesson and it's only more true in business. Don't leave anything broken, left over, or no good lying out or around. Not on desks, tables, or counters, in trucks, warehouses, or closets either. Deal with it—put it away or throw it away—while it's right in your hand. If you wait it's going to nail you!

Pedigree is no guarantee

One of the biggest myths of modern business is the over-reliance on degrees, resumes, and records when it comes to hiring people. Applicants' hands are so full of papers and portfolios they can hardly hold a shovel anymore.

A highly educated and well-bred person can be a real asset, but there's never any guarantee. The barnyard teaches you this over and over. I remember back when registered, pedigreed stock became the big thing. "Papered" stock often did really boost quality or production, but it was by no means the answer to everything. I've often seen plain old "Heinz 57" horses outrun and outwork Thoroughbreds with five-page pedigrees. I've seen "no account" cows produce twice the milk and butterfat of royally registered "name breeds" costing four times as much.

An experience I had when I was thirteen really brought this home to me. I enrolled in the Jerome, Idaho chapter of FFA (Future Farmers of America), unquestionably the best business course I ever had, including all of my college courses. As part of the course we had to pick a project (animal or crop) and buy, care for, and then sell it profitably, keeping records on it all through the year. Me and six or seven others picked pigs as our venture. This meant we had to get a bred sow (female pig) and then raise the babies and sell them. Securing a registered animal for this was the in thing to do, to start your herd right.

Since I didn't have much money and wasn't of legal driving age yet, I was pretty much at my father's mercy. He promised to find me "a good pig" when he went to the livestock sale. Meanwhile, all my buddies were getting set up with the offspring of "Sir Swinesteen VI" or "Miss Swanksow II" type porkers. Finally all of my classmates had their sows, and were enthusiastically entering expenses in record books, and still I remained pigless. Dad continued to assure me that the minute a decent pig came through the sale he'd buy it.

About the time our Ag teacher began giving me anxious looks, Dad came through. As I got off the bus from school I saw the blue stock trailer backed up to the pigpen I'd prepared and I bolted down to behold my project. What a shock! There, looking at her new master with a pure pig-eyed stare, was the biggest, ugliest sow I'd ever seen. Both of her ears had been partially frozen off, her tail was gone, she had a big dent in her right flank, her stomach dragged on the ground, and as near as I could tell she contained all the breeds of my classmates' pigs, with perhaps a few more (and some draft horse) thrown in. She

sure wasn't pedigreed. Crestfallen, I shuffled back to the house, only to hear Dad say, "She's a good pig."

I wouldn't have agreed right then, but was he ever right!

A pig farrows three months, three weeks, and three days from breeding. I had no idea when the surely blindfolded boar had gotten to mine, but in class it was clear that everyone else knew the exact time of breeding and projected birthing date of all theirs. And right on time all their pigs came through. One had five babies, laid on three, and two survived, another had six, of which three died, another had four, of which only one was saved. Finally all of the sows had farrowed except mine, and the best had seven little pigs and lost three.

My pig was entered in my book as "Lady Railroad Tie I" and day after day nothing. Again came anxious looks from my teacher, "Are you sure she's bred?"

"No, but her stomach drags a furrow around the pen." Then, on the most perfect day of the month, she lay down and had fourteen pigs—seven girls and seven boys. She laid on two so I ended up with twelve survivors, more than the whole rest of my class combined! She raised every one of them, and Dad took the six males to pay for the feed, and later I had the six females bred and soon had a profitable herd of seventy. That plain old sow, ugly as sin, no MBA or Ph.D., no high-class blood, just a plain old no-nonsense pig, yielded far more than the Phi Beta Pigga graduates.

Though I do believe in college and attended it myself, it's by no means the most important ingredient of a successful businessperson. Advanced business degrees and specialized certifications won't do the work or indicate how good someone actually is. None of this says or proves one thing about what really counts in business—how hard a person works, how they perform on the battlefield of business, how honest and committed they are. Some of those qualifying papers and credentials may indicate that a person can keep track of things, but it doesn't mean they can make any tracks. What someone can and will do is far more important than the degrees or titles they may have.

My pig herd eventually grew to 120, and all of the lessons learned there would take another book. But one good lesson was enough to start: Don't be taken in by looks or degrees; it's results in business that count!

100 trusts are lost on one bad trade

Lots of deals—trading, buying, and selling—are made in the barnyard. And farmers, like any other businesspeople, have been known to exaggerate a little here and there about how much, how old, or what condition something is in. Used cow and used car salesmen have a few similarities.

A fellow farmer can see a limp, but not always a lump. They can check the teeth, but not always the temper of a critter. They can feel the udder, but don't know the quality of the butter. They can smell the bales of hay on the outside of the stack, but don't know what's inside.

Only truth can create a truly fair trade in business as well as the barnyard. To gain an immediate advantage, we're all tempted to not say all there is to say, not come clean all the way. We may acknowledge the limp because the victim is bound to see that, but we don't mention the lump. But they always find it later, folks, and then suddenly we are short of the stuff called trust. That one lump can contaminate the next one hundred transactions. My dad would never stretch the truth or exaggerate even a little toward the positive in dealing and I always sat back and wished he would, because I knew the others were altering the facts on their side. Dad would even go out of his way to point

out the failings or weak points of the critter, crop, or piece of machinery he was selling.

Looking back on it now, how petty and unimportant a little trade advantage was compared to a lifetime of satisfaction from being known as "honorable;" a man of his word. For years and years now, I've been given deals and opportunities and trust because people dealt with my father and knew that what he said, was the way it was. There were no regrets later.

Too often in business we pad or pare to gain a percentage point or two... only to lose the total of trust. If you have any doubts in a deal or transaction—overpay!

You feed your cows first

Customer relations, without question, is the hardest thing to teach your staff. In business, as anywhere, we're all prone, if not driven, to look out for ourselves first. So getting people to think and act on the principle that the customer or client comes first is next to a miracle. We can come up with signs and slogans and cheerleader chants to assure everyone that, "The customer comes first!" But when you get right down to it most of the time the customers still run a clear second in attention. I've begged my people and done everything in my power to show them how to handle customers to make them feel and know we're there to serve them. But it seems to miss the heart—at best we usually get only the head and hands to care for those who provide our livelihood in business.

Customer service is more than quickly or politely waiting on or taking care of customers—it's delighting them—and sad to say that skill is not in 90 percent of our employees. And as for the 10 percent... how did it get there? Why do some people seem to live and breathe for the customer and even enjoy it? It comes from learning to love and serve early in life. Mine came from the barnyard.

A farmer's livestock is his lifeline, and when a birth occurs in the barnyard, everything is rescheduled around the care of the new arrival. Meals are interrupted, bedtime ignored, dates delayed, fishing trips cancelled, all your personal needs and problems put on hold, until the animal is on its feet and feeling fine. Many unexpected wet, shivering new calves were carried into the house, dried and cleaned off by the stove, and then carefully placed back in the cozy barn on clean straw, and we only felt good about that. When you worked with a team of horses and stopped for any reason you checked and patted your team, and when noon or night came you unhooked or unharnessed those horses, and then fed and wisely watered them before you ate or drank anything yourself—that was the rule of the ranch; no exceptions.

I remember a moment of vanity in my young life once, when I'd scored many heroic points at a ballgame and my parents and I were applauded by many a friend and neighbor. The next night ball practice ran late, and though I usually hitched a ride for part of the six miles home, that night I walked and ran it all so instead of arriving home at 5:30 P.M. I came dragging in at almost seven. I was tired and famished and on the table Mom had left roast, banana Jello salad, fresh homemade bread and raspberry jam. It was too much to pass up and I pulled up a chair to dig in. Suddenly Dad appeared at the door: "Have you fed your animals?" (Remember now, I'm a senior in high school, star athlete, student body president, his offspring, and on the brink of starvation.) "No, in a minute, Dad." "Why you lazy little snot," he said, yanking my chair from under me, and gesturing with his foot toward my fanny as I darted toward the back door, "No real man eats before his cows."

That teaching has been one of the most valuable from Barnyard 101. Your customers and employees come first.

Another rule of the ranch

Another rule of the ranch was self-reliance. If something broke, you didn't return to the house with a dragging face and present it to Dad. Instead, your first thought was, "How am I going to fix this?" Ingenuity was never an option—it was a necessity. If you needed something and it wasn't available, you made it yourself… somehow. During World War II, one of our farmer neighbors blew the engine of his '37 Chevy. You couldn't buy piston rods then, so he found a time-hardened old fencepost and made a rod (yes, out of wood!) and it worked. Even a "jury rig" (baling wire and Band Aid) repair to get the job done was better than being delayed forever, or failing.

When we grew up, this attitude really came in handy. Man, were we resourceful and creative. I had a shop with an anvil, forge, grinders, and other tools, and I could rivet a broken harness, ream out a bearing, or make a replacement arm for a mower support. All of this proved beneficial in my fast-growing cleaning and maintenance business. Many times I outwitted competitors with this kind of resourcefulness and creativity, whether it was in finding ways to recruit new customers or finding (or inventing) the best product or machine to clean something.

You'll need to make a few "rods" now and then, too. We can often make the resources we need, instead of searching all over for them or waiting for them to appear. Just take the time to look around the business "barnyard" for the materials at hand.

Good men go to sleep in soft seats

Ever use an old-fashioned milking stool? When my dad first handed me one, I thought he was kidding. It looked like the letter "T" with half the bottom cut off. You didn't really sit on it, you balanced, and that seemed like adding insult to injury, since milking was no piece of cake anyway. Grandpa, who was always making sage remarks, said, "Good men go to sleep in soft seats," meaning, of course, that the effort of keeping erect on that one-legger would help keep us awake and alert in general.

Decades of experience in the business world now has only confirmed his wisdom. Give someone a plush or soft situation and they do indeed go to sleep on the job. Luxury has no long-range positive value in business; it just softens both our physical and mental muscles.

(By the way, that stool wasn't actually made to make milkers suffer. The limited contact with the ground allowed unlimited shifting of position and angles of approach to save milk, your back, and getting kicked.)

A dull knife is worse than no knife at all

A good pocketknife was one of the marks of a good farm hand. A good pocketknife meant a sharp pocketknife. A dull knife was rated about the same as not having one at all, because it's dull knives that really injure people. A sharp knife may be razor sharp, but since it is sharp we only have to apply minimum effort and pressure when we're using it. And if it does slip, it usually means just a clean slit in our finger or hand. But we have to apply so much force and pressure to a dull knife to make it cut that if and when it slips it really tears us up. Dull is dangerous, and it takes more time to do things. Worst of all, its very presence gives us the illusion that it's doing something, though it isn't. So we keep it around, though we'd be better off seeking better sources. A dull knife just wears out your pocket!

People who don't and won't keep themselves sharp use up space, too, and they give the illusion that because they're there, they must be doing something. But like a dull knife, they aren't much good unless they're able to cut the mustard. Dull costs as much as sharp, causes more blisters and strain, and just plain shouldn't be carried, in the pocket or on the payroll.

Lead ropes and leadership

A good farm and a good business both need a good master; a good leader. But, in the end, any leader is totally dependent on his or her followers. So knowing how to lead kindly and effectively is critical.

1. Be gentle

If you are mean, yanking and jerking on the rope, that which you are leading will rear up and pull back against you.

2. Use the right size rope

If it's too long, there'll be too much slack and you'll find your followers constantly tangled around something. Or they'll have so much leverage they can bolt away, or pull you off the path before you can get them back under control. Too short a rope, and they step on your heels.

Teach them to
3. Respect the rope (the rules)

This is one of the real secrets of leadership with young animals or new employees. On the farm we always tied the animal to a post or other sturdy stationary object for a while and let them tug and yank away at their own discretion. Within hours they figured out that being responsive to the rope was better than fighting it.

Obedience to the ruler is a basic principle of business, and it helps everything run more efficiently. Your rules, the company rules, IRS or OSHA rules, etc.—they may not all be fair or perfect, but they're planted and standing and they have to be followed. Help your employ-

ees to understand that spending their days hating, fighting, and trying to beat the system will only make them bitter, not better. They can tug and pull and fight and yell "foul" all they want, and only end up, like a fighting horse: with no energy and a sore neck.

4. Stay side by side

Keeping an animal close behind you is awkward, plus you can't see it or get any sense of what it's thinking. It can also step on your heels and hang over top of you. If you go side by side, instead, both people and animals will be more willing to be led. You're still in control, but the two of you will feel more like a team. And they'll be willing to put more into it because they'll feel that they have equal billing—equal visibility and equal responsibility for all that you do.

5. Guide, don't drive

If you don't know the difference, you'll suffer lifelong unpopularity with those you work with. It's kind of like the difference between a shepherd and a sheepherder. One leads and guides; the other drives and herds, thinking their power and authority gives them the right to drive people into the ground rather than over it.

When I was ten years old, I was placed on a harrow in a freshly plowed field and handed the reins to a team of workhorses. In case you've never seen them, reins are twenty-foot long belt-size strips of leather that lead to a bit in the mouths of, in this case, three huge horses. As he put the reins in my hand, Dad said, "Remember, you don't drive horses, you guide them, and you do it with a gentle, but firm hand." Then he held his hands over mine and took me on the first round. With just a ripple of the reins and an authoritative "Get up," the horses started moving their load. It seemed so simple—just get started (open a shop and hire some employees), harness them up, and hang on. But no, there was more. "Look," Dad said, "if I hold the reins too tight and keep pulling back on them it hurts the horses and they will fight, and eventually slow down and stop." (And they did.) "If I let the reins go loose the team will go out of control and take off in any old direction, including back to the barn." (And they did.) "The secret is to hold the reins lightly but firmly, so there's enough slack that the animal feels comfortable, yet you can still feel what's going on."

I've found this a perfect formula for leadership in any business.

The secret of early and late

How many successful businesspeople do you know who sleep late and quit early? You'll have to think on that a while and even then you may not come up with one. ALL successful businesses have taken and still take lots of early and late hours. And no place in the world is a better training ground for this particular aspect of business than the barnyard.

The alarm clock back home on the ranch was the screen door of the house opening, and the clumping of Dad's boots as he went out to milk the cows at 5:30 a.m. If you dozed a while and heard the screen door slam a second time when he finished, your goose was cooked! You overslept—a low-down, unmanly thing to do on the farm.

The barnyard has always been a kind of extra or special entity of the farm—the chores here are so vital they're taken for granted. They have to be done but they're so basic they aren't even counted in the regular eight to five workday. You don't do the barnyard chores then, you do them before and after the regular workday. This means a farmer sometimes starts at 4 A.M. and finishes up at seven or eight in the evening. This is every day, too—every morning you show up and every day you do a lot of work. This discipline teaches you that you can do it and establishes habits that last and carry over into any other type of business you might later pursue.

Long hours are required for any business success and when the willingness for extra hours dwindles, so generally does the momentum and prosperity of the operation. "Sleeping in" is a loser practice, and so is throwing in the towel just because you're weary or under the weather. "Company's coming" is no excuse either, for not showing up on the job. No farmer (or businessperson) will last who comes drifting into the barnyard when the sun is wholly up, or who settles back right after dinner and turns on the TV.

Out behind the barn is in full view

There are lots of stories, songs, jokes, and inflated imaginings of what secret, even perverse things have gone on, as country singer Little Jimmy Dickens said, "Out behind the barn." The suggestion is usually that what's done here is mystically hidden somehow, and the party or parties involved get away with it. Out behind the barn was

kind of the back bedroom of the barnyard, where rebellious or inquisitive individuals would sneak to practice swear words, try their first smoke, read a bad book, tell a dirty joke, beat up on little brother, explore sexuality, or practice a sermon, speech, or dance step. The general idea was privacy. But eventually, from an accumulation of comments over the years, I learned that everyone always found out what went on there. They identified the guilty party from a butt or wallet found in the hayloft, or a page of the bad book or coming oration left behind. Or a hired man passing by happened to observe something, or the farmer down the valley got out his binoculars.

Often the guilty party gave himself away. Mom always told us that hanky-panky's biggest tattletale was the person involved—there was always the smell on the breath, the downcast eyes, the slip of the tongue, the shifty feet to brand the bandit. So the back of the barn was actually always in full view, and sneaking around was unquestionably a dumb pastime.

That made a lot of sense to me. Operating in plain sight is a lot more comfortable than trying to hide things in plain brown wrappers. In business or the barnyard, on the farm or in a financial center, the opportunity to shuffle to the shady side is ever present. But if you want to run an operation right, one of your first principles of conduct needs to be that whatever you do out behind the barn (in the back room or break room, in the warehouse or stockroom, in the bar or the janitor closet) will sooner or later be in full view. Consider that before you switch a label, dilute a product, take a bribe, pinch a fanny, undercut a colleague, chug a lug, do a drug, or scribble on a wall. You never get away with it, whether or not your boss or your business partner ever knows about it. If you did it, you own it, and you have to carry it around in how you feel about yourself. A security guard or a Supreme Court judge couldn't punish you worse.

Timing
A critical factor in the barnyard or business

One of my earliest experiences with the importance of precise timing had to do with getting medicine down the throats of sick little calves. It seemed that every so often a newborn calf would have diarrhea, and for some reason it was generally fatal. They couldn't keep food in them and just got weaker and weaker until they died. Dad knew this, and in an attempt to encourage optimism and opportunism in us, would point to the unfortunate little creature and say: "Okay, boys, that calf is yours. If you save it and it grows it will bring you three-hundred dollars some day." That was a deal and we knew what had to be done. There was a big sulfur pill from the vet that had to be administered to that tiny critter, and it wouldn't just willingly gobble it down.

So we had to take a three-foot section of garden hose, insert the pill in one end of it, and carefully put the other end down the calf's throat. The critical part—where the precise timing came in—was that we then had to manage to blow before the calf coughed! I often wondered if the taste of calf breath and sulfur was worth the few calves we ever saved, but the principle of timing I learned there influenced my dealings with clients in all my businesses forever after.

The lesson I learned was "early." If you're late, you always get the bitter pill, and on time even runs risks. But early is always calm and in control. Early, quick action can even compensate for lack of skill or the bad hand you may have been dealt. The time is always right when you're early because it gives you time to adjust. Early even helps with lack of cooperation—being early with an ailing calf or an unhappy customer gives you the best chance of a cure!

When you get stuck, you dig yourself out

Then you'll quit getting stuck! This too was one of the rules of the ranch, and if it were made an unbreakable business code, we'd see a sudden improvement in the economy. Bankruptcy, for example, a legal way to escape a moral obligation, is an example of getting ourselves stuck and then burdening others to get us out. As long as someone else will bail us out, by hand, cash, or legal manipulation, we'll just keep on being careless. We've all been stuck in the mud as kids—like

quicksand it sucked us in and then we cried for Mom, who with some disgust dislodged us, sometimes leaving our boots behind. If you think a little neighborhood mud is bad, you ought to wade through the mud/manure mix in the barnyard.

I got stuck there once, and Mom waded in and fished me out. But from then on it was the rule of the ranch: You got yourself in; you get yourself out. The next time I found myself sinking to my knees in oozy green stuff, I pulled and swayed and bawled, only working myself in deeper. I finally managed to almost struggle out, but with the super suction still gripping my boots I fell over. So I *swam* out in a bath of liquid green manure. A bad scene, but a good lesson. I never took a shortcut across the corral again.

As I grew older, I had to expand the lesson from footwork to farm equipment. I drove the tractor too far into the barn lot and it got stuck up to the axle. Dad shook his head in disbelief and we dug it out; no easy job. The next morning, trying again to get closer in to save a few steps, I buried it clear to the frame. This time the old rule of the ranch was activated—you got it in, you get it out. Dad tossed me a shovel and manure fork. It took hours and I ended up with bleeding hands and an aching back, which added up to brilliant, careful driving after that.

The rule of the ranch went beyond mud puddles: If you broke something, you fixed it; if your fence failed, *you* rounded up the runaway stock; if the tire on something you were using went flat you changed it. At the time this attitude seemed cruel (today it would probably be considered parental abuse), but there's something about answering for our own errors that makes us less likely to make so many. When I grew up and had my own farm, with eight teenage kids and lots of other relatives and friends around, I found out that the rule of the ranch was highly unpopular (especially with my mother-in-law), but I did note a reduction in the number of stuck vehicles after the first time.

Offering gracious and timely help to those who are in need or in deep is an important part of humanity, but if we dig people out repeatedly it only teaches them irresponsibility. We get ourselves in the darndest situations sometimes, and then just stand around and squall like stuck pigs. Don't just stand there, DIG! Allowing people to answer for their actions builds strong muscles and backbones, on the farm or in the corporate headquarters.

All us animals have feelings

My grandfather Ross, a prince of a man who always had a sparkle in his eye and a positive word on his lips, had brought his team of workhorses over to our ranch to help put up hay. It was hard, dusty work, and at the end of one day several of the crew (my uncles, hired men, etc.) happened to be nearby when we were unharnessing the horses. The minute you did that, they generally found a dusty spot, laid down, and rolled gleefully. Grandpa's team (Nebo and Jebo) were pretty old and stiff and one of them picked a spot too close to the electric fence and rolling over, its old legs hit the fence. Our new International fence gave quite a jolt and the horse squealed in fear and pain, and most of the observers roared with laughter. Every time the horse tried to get up, it hit the fence again and would get knocked down by the shock. This was funny to everyone but the horse and Grandpa. He didn't crack a smile as I looked more closely, I saw big tears rolling down his cheeks. This affected me and my concept of kindness forever. Proverbs says that "A good man regards the life of his beast." Grandpa Ross was definitely a good man, and taught his grandson by example.

Those we depend on, human or animal, deserve sensitivity and dignity. There have been times in business when I've been tempted to see the humor in someone's self-inflicted predicament, but it's good to remember that the pain of the situation, like the electric fence, stings that person just the same.

A pat on the head saves a lot of spooking

What makes animals antsy (ready to bolt and run)? I never found all the answers to that, but I did learn that a gentle pat on the neck or head or side saved lots of unnecessary excitement and broken ropes and barn doors. In business this is an equally worthwhile idea when it comes to those who labor with and for you. Many an employee, for reasons we may never know, is antsy at times also, ready to bolt and run. A timely pat on the head here works the same wonders it does in the barnyard.

A manure manual

Manure… both barnyard and business have a lot of it. Even the best business deal comes with some and here's a little barnyard advice on handling it and working with and around it.

Lesson 1:

"Horse manure"—this phrase or a similar one has been used for centuries to describe what is also called "hot air." And truly about half the verbiage used to sell us things, or coax or convince us to do something could be genuine horse droppings. Those who are into manure in business are under the illusion that it has a lot of value, as it "fertilizes things for a better deal." That may be true to a degree, but all farmers and gardeners know it also contains all sorts of weed seed and after you spread it around you will see sprout heaven. (And it won't be anything you wanted to see sprouting, either.)

Most horse manure is heavy and smelly when it's fresh and that is a poor time to handle it or weigh it in your business decision-making. Handle manure in business like we farmers handled the real stuff. We kicked the pile apart a little and let it dry, and in a day or two it became as light, pleasant, and inoffensive as potpourri. Its essence was all that was left now, and it could be useful, too.

In our rural schoolyard we had the finest of all high jump pits, with a cushioning at the bottom superior to any foam rubber or air balloon. It was (all three feet deep of it) dried horse manure. It was almost heavenly to sink down into and no matter how much of it we retained in our pockets, socks, ears, or nose there were no negative aftereffects. When you hear horse manure in a conversation or presentation, kick it apart and let it dry out a few days. Before long the few facts left will become clear, dry, and easily used.

Lesson 2:

When you hang around animals in a corral, or people in an office, or anywhere there are manure dispensers willing and able to dispense it, you're bound to end up with some on you.

Manure, like gossip and office politics, is best dealt with immediately. If you clean it off or haul it off right away, it comes off easily and has little aftereffect. If you ignore it and just leave it on you, you spread it all over and end up stinking up the place.

And if you ignore it and leave it around, it gradually rots and destroys your fenceposts and the very structure of your barns and sheds, etc. (or your corporation).

Lesson 3:

In fifty years in business I've probably attended at least 14,000 meetings of one kind or another, and reflecting back on them all now I'd say that was probably about 10,000 too many. Now that I'm an experienced executive, I realize there's a barnyard lesson I should have applied sooner: *Where many cows are gathered together, much manure results.*

No matter what kind of business you're in, think about this before you call up a "quick meeting." Well-planned, well-directed, well-motivated businesses don't need lots of meetings. Most meetings are twice too long and twice too many.

Lesson 4:

If you don't clean up the manure, it gets in the milk.

The essence of eliteness in barnyard manners was to bring the house milk in without a speck of foreign matter in it. Sometimes the milk (if you were a good, fast milker) would have a head of foam on it, which made it look white and clean when you presented it to Mom. However, after it was strained, an examination of the straining cloth, which collected anything that got into the milk, told a different tale.

I struggled for years to bring in clean milk. Dad's was always immaculate, and mine always seemed to yield pieces of hair, straw, dried

doo-doo, etc. I couldn't seem to avoid getting something in the milk and in fact I never did fully master it. But I did learn another business basic here: If you don't clean up the manure (any problems) before you start, it always gets in the business. Some people think that a business can operate with a muddle of present and future problems floating around in there; "It'll never show." But it will show on that straining cloth, and you'll know it when your product or output is downgraded from Grade A to B or C. And worse yet, if it's been in there long enough and becomes liquid like the milk, you *can't* strain it out.

Last lesson:

When it's deep, wear boots!

Leave things that are none of your business ALONE!

Here's another real business basic: don't stick your nose (or anything else) in places where it doesn't belong.

How many times in the barnyard, messing with things we were told to leave alone, did we end up in a bad way?

That nest of hornets, for example. They were up there keeping to themselves out on that branch, but we had to get a long stick and climb up there and poke, probe, and punch until the nest dropped and we had to run for it. Some of us weren't fast enough, and full of welts and stings we ran to the house for pain relief. As we bawled, Mother darned those nasty hornets for stinging her little babies. (We never bothered to mention how hard we worked to earn those stings, of course.)

Ditto for our bad experiences with snakes and knives, the baby bull we just had to tease and the calf medicine we just had to taste, the electric fence we had to touch, the knothole we had to stick our finger in, the neighbor's apple orchard we just had to sneak into. We got into a lot of grief when we didn't mind our own business.

Though it took me quite a few stings, bites, shocks, paddlings, and groundings to learn, I finally did learn not to ask for trouble. Which includes staying out of other people's personal affairs. I never read anyone's mail or open their drawers, or listen to their calls, for example, even if they work for me. I just keep out of their personal and private lives and it feels good. Things that are none of your business can consume you. Minding your own business leaves a lot fewer messes to mend.

New is nice, but...

The Ohio farmers call it "New Paint Fever;" out West we call it "New Pickup Itch." The columnists call it "Keeping up with the Joneses" and the preachers, vanity. Whatever you call it, it's generally bad judgment.

Some farmer down the road buys a new tractor, cornplanter, combine, pickup or posthole digger and that shiny new paint and new vehicle smell drives all the rest of us wild. Whether we need it or not, all the rest of us want something new, too. Many times back on the ranch when we were working in the barnyard (spring or fall seemed to be the most susceptible seasons), a neighbor would drive in with a new truck. The doors slammed good and tight, there was no manure dripping out the back, or hoof or post dents in the bed. There were no cracks on the windows, the upholstery was unblemished, and there wasn't a speck of rust, just shining metal everywhere. Gads, it sure stimulated the vanity gland.

If you happened to have had a good year it was double jeopardy, and then there was the "image" or prestige problem, including with your kids, who would run over to that spanking new black-tired truck and pet it and walk all around it. Add up all those symptoms and you can see why new paint fever has sent lots of otherwise successful farmers into bankruptcy.

Dad never caved in, though I was given to jealousy, and my brother even brought it up, "Why we didn't have new?" Dad's answer was that unnecessary debt is real dumb, and that our stuff (every single piece of which we bought used, usually from a paint fever farmer selling out) worked fine. Our crops were in faster and our yield was as good, and that is one of our biggest goals in business, to see through new paint and keep the focus on function. Good farm equipment and tools can last and function well for decades. The old tractor may be ugly and have a few nicks and weld knots on its skin,

but it runs just as well and plows just as deep and fast as the new one (which is generally about the same as the old, only with new paint and a pretty emblem).

> "The newest piece of equipment I've got is seventeen years old...."

New paint fever—wanting and getting what you don't need and can't afford—has not only put many businesses under, but broken marriages and caused suicides and depression. Learning to live well with what you've got is one of the great, great disciplines of business. A tough one to balance with a big ego, though—it helps to remember that there'll be dents, scrapes, and manure running down and out the tailgate before long on anything new!

By hand?

Another valuable thing I learned in my farm days was how much you could get done by hand if you had to, if you simply kept at it. For example, keeping cattle all winter in corrals would result in a buildup of a mixture of manure and bedding straw that had to be removed each spring. The old way was by hand, with a manure fork. It would be dug out and tossed on a wagon, taken to the fields and spread by hand for fertilizer. Many of our neighbors spent hours working with big loaders on the front end of a tractor. We had no loader, and I remember getting thirty-two loads by hand one day and in a week of off-and-on work we had the whole corral cleaned by hand—great exercise. Likewise, while neighbors had automatic bale loaders, we did ours by hand. We had more hay and always had our hay up first.

Forty years later, a dump truck dumped a load of gravel on the road at my ranch and needed to go get another load. He asked where my backhoe or Bobcat ($55 per hour to rent) was. When I told him I'd be spreading it by hand with a shovel and wheelbarrow, he laughed. By the time he returned with the other load it was finished.

You might be surprised how much can still be done most efficiently by hand. One day, for instance, we had three postholes to dig on the corral at my ranch. My son said, "Let's use the automatic posthole digger, Dad. It can dig a hole a minute." I told him each hole would only take ten minutes by hand. "But that's thirty minutes of work," he said. "Yes, but it's faster than the hour it will take to put the digger on the tractor, and then take it off again, so we'll save at least a half hour doing it by hand."

Sometimes a primitive, five-minute effort on hands and knees makes a lot more sense than fifty minutes setting up a machine that "does all the work."

Force fails

This biggest lesson of the barnyard is unquestionably the basic rule for handling any situation anywhere—forcing fails. In business as well as the barnyard we are constantly moving, re-situating, transferring, even herding those providing our livelihood. We know exactly where we want them to go and why and when. Seldom do they know or even care about the reasons, they only sense that they are being guided or pushed.

The first time I can remember being sent to "Go get the cows," I carried a big threatening stick and stayed close to the fence in case one should decide to come after me. I walked a mile to the end of the pasture and got behind the cows and drove them to the barn. They all stopped then and just stood there by the open barn door, so I charged them, yelling and hitting my club on the ground in an attempt to push them all through that opening. They just milled around and bunched more closely together. I was insulted by now so I started throwing rocks and raving "You dumb cows…." When I got too close they panicked and bolted and all ran past me right back to the end of the pasture a mile away.

I went back to the house in defeat, only to be sent right back out again. In increasing ill temper I blamed those "stupid stock" for the third mile I had to walk now. I got them all back to the barn again, and again they just stood there. And again I began the same process of force and intimidation to try and get them to accept the door as their destination. I had them about ready to bolt again when Dad, who'd been watching out the window, came outside. He pulled me back and told me just to stand aside for a while so those cows could quit looking at and worrying about me. One or two of the animals would find the door, he said, and then the others would follow. And indeed it worked, like magic.

Likewise, I watched three men trying to load a prize bull into a truck once. The bull wasn't about to get into that truck and he didn't even want to go into the chute. Somehow they pushed and prodded the animal to the base of the chute, and now that they had him almost cornered, the three of them—one from the top, one from behind, and one from the side—started poking, slapping, yelling, threatening, banging, and shoving against the steel posts to "coax" the animal up the ramp into the chute. They were impatient and the bull was stubborn (in case you wondered where the expression "bull-headed" came from). The bull did have some options:

1. Go into the truck.
2. Stay there and continue to get beaten and terrorized.
3. Jump over the side.
4. Turn around and trample the bully behind him.

This bull chose course #3—he reared up on his hind legs and hooked his front legs over the top pole and under the pressure of at least 1500 pounds, it snapped. Then he leaped over what was left. To make matters worse the ill-tempered man on the side struck the bull several times with a shovel as it departed. The thoroughly intimidated, but now free animal ran like a freight train through expensive small corrals, gates, and fences before it headed out to the range for some peace, ignoring all the threats and curses from his assailants now far behind him.

We've all watched business leaders do the same thing to subordinates to force them into a new slot or assignment. Their clubs and verbiage may be more camouflaged than the bull loaders', but it's just as deadly. And it's just as likely to get someone to rear up on his hind legs and make a bad decision for all concerned. Often the open door or chute is actually the way to something better, but the forcers fail to make that clear to the forcees and give them a little slack and liberty to let it sink in. The bull, for example, was being transferred to service a pastureful of fresh little heifers. Had he known that he might have jumped right in the truck without the chute.

Bulls are hard to talk to, but humans aren't. So tell them about the pasture and back off and eat an apple—95 percent of them will run right up the chute on their own. By the time I was twenty-one I was an expert animal loader and herder. It was all a matter of forgetting force and letting the individual find the opening and use their willingness instead of my bossiness.

Standing asleep

I'll never forget the day I discovered horses can and do sleep standing up.

I walked up to a horse and saw that his head was down and his eyes were closed, even though every so often his back twitched in the usual fly-defensive manner. I touched him lightly on the shoulder and said "Hi Star," and that usually gentle creature jumped like a magnet to metal. He snorted, made a couple of leaps that shook all the cobwebs off the rafters, and then gave me a dirty look.

Years later, hiring and working with my cleaning and contracting crews, I found that there are plenty of "sleeping horse" people. They're there on the job every day, on their feet, on the computer, or in a nice office chair, and they may even twitch their hide every so often, but they aren't actually doing anything. The workforce is full of sleeping horses who only do about two hours of work a day, but look busy for eight.

The barnyard teaches you to spot and keep the real producers. If it's you who dozes on the job, bear in mind that they make glue out of old sleeping horses, or ship them to Paris for steaks—draw your own conclusions.

Animals in heat do dumb things

When it comes to sex, barnyards have some class. Animals reproduce without making a big thing of it. They don't photograph a couple

of cows going at it, and then gather at the barn at a late hour and watch it, panting and snorting. Animals only have brief moments of obsession with their procreative drives, which we referred to as being "in heat." For a day or so every month or so you'd see them whinnying and prancing around with flaring nostrils, willing to mount anything that moved. Cattle are rather frisky at such moments (whence probably arose the word horny)—they nuzzle and sniff around until they cool off or get a roll in the hay, whereupon they go right back to their normal everyday life of eating grass and hay.

Sex is decently simple in the barnyard, which is more than you can say about most of the business world. A horse in heat may break a gate or jump a fence to gallop to romance, but in too many offices people are in heat all the time. And workplaces are full of posters, pictures, postures, perfumes, suggestive clothes, conversations, and millions of racy jokes a day, all designed to turn up the heat and keep it up. If American businesspeople would use three-quarters of the energy and brainpower to work that they now use to lust, they could melt world competition forever in a month.

I was at the head office once of a Fortune 500 company consulting on building design to ease maintenance, and the conversation swung to the "open office" concept. "It's killing our output," management told me.

"Really? All the studies show it to be a definite upgrade," I answered. That might be true in theory, they told me, but it didn't take into account the carnal nature of humankind. "Watch this," they said, as a stunning blonde, her clothes appearing to have been painted on with a spray gun, sauntered down the aisle of 150-feet of desks, almost every man stopped, and didn't just give her a warm glance, but followed her progress for at least three minutes, savoring the whole 150-feet.

Do you know how much production time is lost when forty people—men or women—stop and watch and work up a sweat? People in heat in business may not break fences, but they do break rules and boundaries and forget schedules in their quest for a little foreplay and excitement. Creatures in heat have very poor judgment. We can survive and compensate for one or two days a month in the barnyard, but in the boardroom it sure sabotages the ends and goals of business.

Sex is great, but if animals were in heat all the time like us humans, barnyards would be out of business fast. There's a difference between reproducing and *producing!*

Big udders generate poor judgment

While we're on risqué subjects, let me point out that choosing premium stock can be deceptive. The milk cow with the biggest udder, for instance, isn't necessarily the best. A lot of other criteria need to be considered such as back and hip construction, height, lineage, intelligence, temperament, production record, etc. On the farm or in the office, buying for the bustline is a good way to go bust. It may attract a lot of attention and get a lot of mention, but it'll rarely gain you the kind of help you really want and need.

Not all bulls breed

Business is full of "bulls" or at least would-be bulls of both sexes—executives, managers, supervisors, vice presidents—all kinds of big, tough individuals who have a title and position, and maybe tenure and a window in their office, too. So they strut, prance, snort, toss their weight around, and bellow like a barnyard bull. Not all bulls breed, however, even though they may have the build and the pedigree and proper facilities and even assume the proper position.

How long has business bought and fed young new executive bulls and introduced them to the herd, but no new ideas or progress are born in the spring? Stockholders are easy to fool, but stock owners aren't, so this is one of the first lessons of the barnyard. If your bulls don't breed, get rid of them (a principle that could save many businesses this hour).

Perhaps I'm more sensitive to this "production" principle than some, but you see I've lived both extremes. By the age of thirteen or fourteen I'd already made money on hogs and heifers; I had $780 saved. In 1951, that was a third of a year's salary. Now Dad was buying some baby Hereford bulls and he said, "A good mature bull, two years down the road, can be worth $1800-$150,000. Do you want to invest in one?" Being bullish, even then, I said I did. And so when a herd of registered, "Larry Domino/Republic" baby bull calves was unloaded, Dad said, "Go pick one you want." I sat on the corral a long time to look them over. A cute little curly-faced one finally caught my eye (my after-the-fact advice now is never pick a bull that looks like Richard Simmons). Two years later, when the other bulls were making hay with the heifers, mine was in the corral eating hay. He brought $400 as hamburger.

There are thousands and thousands of "hamburger" executives around who think they are studs and steaks and get paid and positioned that way. They might be bulls in every other respect—looks, books, and bellows—but if they don't multiply the profits you've got some subtracting to do.

Down wind is a bad place to be

Another thing you learn quick on the farm is that eating someone else's dust is no fun. If you stay downwind from any activity you'll eventually get the fallout. If you get on the wrong side of someone pitching hay, sharpening a sickle, shoveling sand, or even spitting off the side of a wagon, you'll get it—everything blows in your face.

Proper positioning is the answer for less abuse in life, and once you figure that out, you'll have a big business advantage, too. Almost anywhere (on the playing field, at a concert, in a line, even at the dinner table), where you put and keep yourself is like those three biggest success factors in real estate: Location! Location! Location! Position is even more important than location, because *we* determine and control our position—whether we sit, stand, operate, etc.—above, below, in front, or behind.

Don't park under the rafters

How many times in business do we complain about being "taken"—abused, ill treated, if not pooped on? Plenty. We do have a choice in the matter, namely, we can choose who we deal with and where we position ourselves. Where we situate ourselves largely determines the soiling and assault level. In the barnyard one of our earliest lessons was: "Don't park under the rafters." If you left the tractor, truck, or tools in that vulnerable spot you'd always find them well-decorated with bird manure. Careless, inconsiderate sparrows, pigeons, or even chickens roosted on those rafters and dropped smeary little bombs on the instrument panels, the seats, and the steering wheel. The longer you left your things there the worse it was. The business message here is don't park under or around people who support the source of soiling.

Greedy, pushy animals

Greedy, pushy, disobedient animals are always the first to go... to the slaughterhouse! Some animals are just plain mean; they never change. You keep them by themselves, you put them with other, gentler, nicer animals, you give them extra food and attention and they're still ornery. They'll smash or tear things up, try to nip you, cause trouble any chance they get. They crowd all the other animals away from the trough, bowl, or manger and after they've had third and fourth helpings they stand around and grunt or whine for a fifth and sixth.

Every farmer loves and depends on his animals, but here, as anywhere, enough is enough. After a long series of reprimands, warnings, and attempted adjustments, and still no change, it's off to the baloney factory. Even registered (MBA degreed) milk cows with a life expectancy of ten or more years have been known to be packed off to the final meat locker in the sky for being greedy, pushy, and disobedient.

This fits the realities of business perfectly. Yes it's shape up, or literally be shipped out.

Facing the chores

Rural life had two main categories of work when I was growing up: field work and "the chores." The chores were the same old dependable duties, kind of like the cooking, cleaning, and laundry of the barnyard. You did the chores before or after the fieldwork, which generally meant very early or very late. How you faced the early chores seemed to set the pattern for the day. Our folks always taught us this was solely our choice. A "bad day" had little or nothing to do with the events of the day; it was determined solely by your attitude.

What was our attitude? I'd wake up before dawn in the bunkhouse hearing Dad or Grandpa singing or whistling, or shouting encouragement to the cows as they served up the bales. Some mornings Dad would come out of the house, walk out into the barnyard, stop, sigh, look all around him, beat on his chest a couple of times, then take a deep breath and say, "Man, isn't it great to be alive!"

This was the approach to work I learned, so it was a real shock when I left home and saw what so many people elsewhere did: drag themselves out of bed, down a couple of cups of coffee to get their eyes open, and then grump, groan, and pout their way out to the "barn." That's like deciding right then that the day is going to be miserable. It reminds me, too, of how Dad told us you know when a horse is going to kick you—his ears are laid back, his head is down, and he has a squinty-eyed frown.

We, not the chore or challenge ahead, solely determine whether we will cherish a day or chuck it.

Weeds pull easier when small

A business, like soil in a barnyard, field, or garden, grows all kinds of unwanted weeds. You don't have to plant weeds in the ground, or cultivate problems in a business. Both will appear and flourish by themselves and if you handle weeds and business problems the same you'll enjoy a more trouble-free operation.

If you leave a problem to grow bigger in a business, like a weed, it will root deeper into its environment. Then it is not only hard to remove, but when and if it is finally pulled it will often take part of whatever good is nearby with it.

Waiting to weed:
1. Allows weeds to get bigger and tougher
2. Enables them to spread and seed more weeds everywhere
3. Uses up nutrients, energy, and water (your resources)
4. Chokes out desirable entities, or keeps them from thriving
5. Encourages pests and insects (such as lawyers)
6. May require the application of poisonous remedies
7. Pollutes the landscape/surroundings—makes things ugly

Weeds, like problems in a business, can be cut or pulled easily in the beginning, but letting either weeds or wrongs go means "wait and weep."

A well-painted barn earns praise

When I was a child, we moved into a farm community where we didn't know anyone, and as we drove back and forth moving in our household goods and farm equipment we passed all of our new neighbors' places. Who were the ones we most wanted to meet, the ones we remembered best when they came over to introduce themselves? The people with the painted barn. The barn seemed to be the necktie

of the whole agricultural outfit. That single thing—a painted barn—seemed to establish the fact that the owner cared.

Anything that gets hard use gets worn and tired and eventually a little shabby looking. Our cars, desks, tools, buildings, and yes even we ourselves can get nicked, scuffed, and warped, chipped and faded and saggy, and we no longer look so good, though we may still be putting out a pretty good product. Appearance may indeed be mere superficial vanity in some situations, but in business it's often the key to capturing the customer to begin with. Shabbiness speaks twenty-four hours a day, and it doesn't need a voice to say:

1. I don't care.
2. I'll accept anything.
3. I used to be a lot better than I am now.

Appearances can and will suggest your attitude and condition to a passer-by and make a difference when they decide whether to use you or not.

You and your place look better, feel better, and last longer when decently presented. A coat of paint isn't an attempt to fake people out, or to hide the old and fading. It's a banner of your standards, a way of letting people know you appreciate what you have, and that you're willing to make an effort, pay a price, to preserve it. Look around your business or home right now and consider for a minute what a simple gallon or two of paint, or even a bucket of soap and water, could do. I complimented a woman recently on how nice she looked at all times, no matter what the hour or the situation, and her reply summarizes my point here nicely: "I believe any old barn looks better with a little paint."

Never wait until you're "out" to replenish

The most basic of all business wisdom is to never run out of stock or inventory, yet not keep so much on hand that it rots, or eats your cash flow. Running out is costly, and it has a ripple effect. When you run out, the customer or the cow goes without and neither forget it, even if you give them double rations later. Running out labels you incompetent, a poor planner, no matter how good your excuse (the weather, shipping delays, etc.). What flashes through your mind when someone doesn't show or arrives late and tells you they ran out of gas? Incompetent! Poor planner! Would you ever go back to a caterer who ran out of food in the middle of the reception? Or a hospital that ran out of bandages? If you want to triple your time and trouble on a job, run out of paint or nails or paper when you're almost done. Being caught out of anything you need is just plain bad for business. No one cares why, even if the reason is 100 percent truth. They only want what they came for—and your job is to supply it.

We fed stock out of our own granary and when I was ten or twelve years old I ran out of chopped grain on the worst thirty-below-zero day of the year. I did all the feeding so Dad had no idea how much we had left until I came in with cows bellowing in the background, and announced, "Dad we're out of grain." "Why, you poor simp," he said, "you never wait until you're out to add more! We could have chopped grain two weeks ago while it was warm, now...." It was miserably cold and the cows were starving and I knew from their Guernsey glances they hated me for my ineptness.

> When you're OUT of something you are IN for punishment—physical, emotional, and even social, from all those onlookers who are wondering who would be dumb enough to not bring or have enough.

Even this wasn't as bad as the day I ran out of twine (the rope that holds bales together) right in the middle of baling, on a prime haying day. The whole operation ground to a halt, and the hay dried out and lost a lot of its cow appeal as we went to town and waited, etc., to get more. Another time I ran out of Bag Balm (50¢ a can then), an ointment you put on the cows' udders and teats to keep them soft and milkable. So old Bossy's teats got sore and cracked and bled, and she kicked me.

I don't know whether it was that kick, or the regrets from running out of shells the time we ran across eighty quail in one covey, running out of money when the Ted Williams Special Edition Slugger was on sale, or running out of clean shirts the night of the senior victory dance at school, but somewhere early on I learned the principle of replenishment. In short, making sure I had enough and then some.

No advice about business run-outs is complete without the mention of money. It's especially bad to wait until you're out of *this* to replenish it. Have you ever stopped to think what a helpless, begging position being moneyless puts you in, at any age? "Broke" breaks more than the line between black and red on the balance sheet. It causes all kinds of compromises and inconveniences, breaks spirits and relationships, and destroys confidence.

Running out doesn't simply leave you without until you get some more. Running out is the most effective way known to rack up unnecessary expenses, and encourage the more dangerous kinds of ingenuity. And those who run out, and don't know they're out until they're out, really put themselves on the outs with bosses, associates, and of course the cows (customers).

If you don't know what the weather is going to be, overdress

This is a related principle that has saved my hide hundreds of times. If you're not sure what the weather's going to be, *overdress!*

Nothing is worse than being out in the barn or up on the mountain, at the ballpark or on the beach, and COLD! Miserably cold! You'd kill for mittens and a coat, or a sweater, or for that matter even just a nice warm shirt. Why didn't I bring one? I could have taken it off if I got too hot.

This is an important, but easy management skill to master. If you don't know what you need, "more" is smart. Bring more, you can always take it back. Returning a few extras at your convenience, in your own good time sure beats scrounging around when you're short, with no time to spare.

Know where you are!

What's the #1 reason for financial failure at home as well as in business? People don't know where they are.

Let's take a look at this down on the farm. Many farmers Dad and I knew lost their farms or were gradually squeezed out when farming got more sophisticated and competitive. Many of them milked cows, receiving a big milk check every month that came just in time to make payments and buy groceries. The check was such a boon that the expenses that went into getting that check were seldom charted. One farmer, for example, was getting a $2300 milk check. He milked morning and night and fed and catered to those cows constantly. Every month he and his family went deeper in debt, but that milk check kept coming. Finally they lost the farm and moved to the city and got jobs in stores and factories.

Still disturbed by what had happened (because he was actually smart and had worked his butt off), the farmer finally did something too many of us managers never get around to, and that was to calculate the true cost of producing that milk check.

He raised the hay he fed, so he'd never figured it into the expenses—it was just there. But the cost of raising the hay, cutting and baling and transporting it, the twine to tie the bales, etc., was cash out of pocket. Because he didn't sell the hay, he fed it, until now he never knew that his hay cost per month was $2000! His vet bills per month averaged $80; the grain for the herd was over $300 a month; the utilities for the barn, milking equipment, and manure disposal system another $150; taxes on the barn came in at $20 a month; the payment on the automatic milker $101; udder salves and other miscellaneous cow care items ran about $50 a month; and the pasture he irrigated with a pump cost him over $300 a month. And then, because at least one cow died every year, there was a replacement cost to be considered (easily overlooked because they reproduce for free, right?) Wrong! The cost of replacements—he'd always gotten loans for that—averaged out to $160 a month.

It never occurred to him that these expenses were quietly mounting up every month. They were invisible to him because he never actually received a statement or invoice detailing their cost in black and white. When he added all of the expenses for the dairy together they came to $3,361 a month! Bottom line: He was **losing $1,061 a month**, not counting all of the labor involved in all of this!

Many of us are spending much more than we take in. However, because when those big checks come in we get some short-range relief, we don't really see the long-term deficit. That deficit slowly but surely adds up and catches up to us. Always take the time to figure out, and know where you are!

"Too many irons in the fire"

This old expression is still used today as an excuse to drop the ball, or to describe an "over-busy" person. Is having "too many irons in the fire" really negative?

In my early life, I worked with not the proverbial, but the real irons in the fire that originated this cliché. All of our cattle on the ranch had to be "labeled," or branded, and this was usually done in the spring. We'd build a mighty fire near the corralled critters to generate a good bed of glowing coals, into which we thrust our branding irons. The irons were four feet long, with the rancher's "initials" on the end. Then the cows and calves were wrestled to the ground or clamped in a chute. An iron was left in the fire until it was white hot, then snatched up and pushed against the critter in the spot (right shoulder, left rump,

etc.) assigned by the brand commissioner, permanently marking the animal's hide. This looked painful to me, but the old cowboys told me it didn't hurt much because it just singed the hair and the very outside layer of the skin. The cows, with their bellowing, disagreed.

During a "brand" the iron would cool off, and so have to be reheated. If you had only one iron everyone had to wait around until it was ready to use again. Good sense told us that if we had more than one in the fire and rotated them, the branding process would be greatly expedited. Since as a youngster I was the head flunky, I generally tended the irons. Especially when two or more ranches were branding together, whenever a cowboy got a wrong or cold iron he would come out with the old accusation: too many irons in the fire. Of course the more irons and the more different brands involved, the greater the challenge and chance of confusion.

But having lots of irons in the fire is an efficient and even environmentally desirable (you only need one fire) way to go. The problem wasn't the number of irons in the fire, it was the handling of them. When irons are stuck anywhere at random and all twenty handles sticking out of the fire look the same, you can understand a certain propensity to error. Instead of less irons, you need to send your dull "cowboys" to the Dodge City memory seminar, or to mark the handles of the different brands in some way. Or (the system I eventually worked out) the Bar B irons should always be laid in the west side of the fire, Rocking Rock ranch on the east side, and Aslett Acres on the north, and no matter how many irons there are in the fire they won't get mixed up.

Having lots of irons in the fire—a lot going on—at all times is the way it should be. The answer isn't fewer irons, it's organizing them better.

P. S. In case you're still worrying about those calves, we've all gone to using a paste on the irons that marks the animal just as well with zero pain. "Too many irons in the pot," however, doesn't have quite the same ring.

South Forty

No cool place to work

As one of my farmer neighbors said as he and his crew were repairing a baler in the blistering heat of a machine shed, "It's hard to find a cool place to work."

I'm often criticized for not noticing that it's too hot or too cold to work—and that too is a blessing from the barnyard. There you took

what you got by way of weather, and you often had to work the hardest on the hottest days of the year. Moaning and groaning didn't make it any cooler, so you quit noticing the temperature and the elements and did the job. You just walked outside, or into the room, and accepted it.

Our production level around the farm wasn't determined by the weather, but by what needed to be done. Days when it was so hot out on those desert fields you could hardly breathe, Dad, Mom, we kids, and even Grandad hit the chores the same as if it were 70 degrees. Sometimes the wind was strong all day, blowing bits of straw, manure, and sand into your face so hard that it stung—you just adjusted your eyes to a squint and kept going. One year we had a grasshopper plague you wouldn't believe, and we were haying in 105-degree weather. As you rode the tractor (no closed cabs in those days) through the field, thousands of hoppers would leap up and many would strike you in the face like miniature missiles—man, they hurt. We'd whine and Dad would say, "Well, you dummies, hold your hand in front of your face and get on with it." If you were hit by a quick hailstorm out in the fields, unprotected, those icy little missiles would about tear your ears off. Lightning, too, strikes both at the barn and in business. It's part of the risk of living, so just duck till it's over and then get on with it.

Likewise, when cold weather comes and the climate gets forbidding, sales drop and most businesses slow down and suffer (unless you run a ski lift). But cold is just a condition, not necessarily a negative. We learned in the barnyard that when it's time to work, unless you're a chemist or gardener, temperature is irrelevant. Ten below only meant that you dressed warmer and started earlier. You didn't wait for things to "warm up." The cold had a crispness that stimulated blood flow and a blanket of new snow was never a reason to not do something.

I remember one Saturday morning when it was thirty-two below. Dad jumped up enthusiastically after breakfast, rubbed his hands together and said, "No sense sitting around in the house like a bunch of lounge lizards. Let's go pick the manure down so the calves can reach the manger." And we did. As we worked to lower the built-up manure where the

feeder calves usually stood, little chunks of flint-hard frozen manure flew in all directions. It was downright stimulating to know that our hands and feet would freeze up if we stopped. It was a clear, bright day and what a glorious time we had—it was refreshing and good to be doing something.

Years and years of business profit and success have come from that corral classroom. When I was twenty-five, for example, I drove 360 miles in severe weather to clean a single building (it only took an hour) in Jackson Hole—I had to honor our contract and was suddenly left without an employee there to do it. When I was thirty-five, the temperature dropped to sixty below at the Sun Valley resort I was in charge of maintaining. Almost eight feet of compressed snow was dangerously weighing down the roofs of some of the buildings. It was way up high and it had to be removed by hand and no one wanted to do it. Thanks to our barnyard conditioning, it was just a nice afternoon's work for me and a couple other farm kids. And when I was forty and a major account cooled down and gave our industry the cold shoulder, I was able to not only survive but prosper.

Things may sting or go numb or break when it's cold, but icicles don't authorize inactivity.

Don't let weather decide whether

You don't have to be in business long to know that there are fair, cloudy, warm, hot, rainy, and chilly as well as cold days, yet in most businesses the same things still need doing. Real winners progress and prosper no matter what the weather.

Weather may force some limitations on us, but it can't affect our conduct or affairs unless we let it. Weather is so easy to outwit. Get up earlier, work later or harder, wear more or less, or change your project or workstation. Never worry about the weather, or use it as an excuse, or tie your production to it. Just put on a thicker sweater or a thinner t-shirt and do what you have to do!

Milking manners

Lesson 1:
If you keep your head in the job, you'll seldom get kicked

When I was growing up, all milking was hand milking. Before I was old enough to milk, this milking business looked simple enough. I observed that the milker person would sit on a little stool next to the cow, put the bucket under the animal, and squeeze and pull on the teats and the bucket would fill. When my day to try it came, I got kicked again and again.

Finally, Grandpa put his hand on the back of my head and shoved my face into the flank of the cow. "Now Donald, if you keep your head in your job, instead of gandering around, you can feel the kicks coming. Push your head harder and the cow won't kick you." And it worked!

I have no doubt today, as I watch businesses operate, that those who tend and caretake and administrate business from afar are the ones getting kicked all the time. Those who keep their heads buried in their work and responsibility and aren't "gandering around" are the ones who end up with the most cream.

Lesson 2:
Even nice cows will kick!

So many times I was told, before setting my milking stool under a cow, that she was a nice gentle cow… only to be, in the process of milking, soundly kicked. The problem was never with the cow, it was the milker (me), who managed to pinch, pull, push, startle, or somehow offend the cow. This is a perfect parallel to the customer who "kicks"—they too have been somehow pinched, pulled, pushed, startled, or offended.

I corrected my milking manners and the kicking stopped, and it works the same in business!

Borrowing costs

Observing adults when I was a kid, I discovered a seemingly perfect way to get something you wanted or needed but couldn't afford to buy—you borrowed it. Free access, or so it appeared. It just took a tiny bit of effort to ask, and then you had it. What a deal!

There might be a catch, my conscience told me, and then sure enough one afternoon, while we were stacking hay in the corral area, a neighbor drove in and asked if he could borrow something. I don't recall what it was, but Dad said yes and the neighbor drove off with it. When Dad returned he was muttering away about how dumb it was to borrow the item.

"Berkley drove ten miles to get that, and he's got to drive ten miles to return it. It's old and it'll probably break and he'll have to fix or replace it. Or he'll forget he's got it and when we need it we'll have to call and then maybe go over and get it. It would have been cheaper in the long run just to buy and give him one. Mutter, mutter, mutter...."

Not only did Dad have a whole list of negatives about borrowing, but as time went on I realized that (except for some intrafamily exchanges), we and the other more successful farmers around never borrowed things. It was mainly the strugglers who did. These facts stuck with me and in the business world the principle has proven true. What you borrow, you have to return, and there is always an "interest" or cost of some kind involved. In most cases the smartest and cheapest course, in terms of both time and money, is to go get your own.

That "interest" of borrowing has bankrupted innumerable people. Not just the actual dollars of compound or per annum interest, but all of the extra little trips and nuisances involved. Owning isn't selfish or capitalistic, it's essential sometimes, if you want to control your time and money. Only then will you always be able to choose the time and the place and the conditions, and keep yourself out of debt and unobligated. The borrower, even of a rake or a shovel, is in debt, you see. They owe, and they'll have to be available to lend something of their own, or do a return favor, at some undoubtedly inconvenient time in the future. They're usually gathering demerits, too, because whoever had it, had it because they needed it. When it's been borrowed they won't have it when they need it!

The local district office of the Boy Scouts, twenty-five miles away, has hiking, camping, and sports equipment available to loan out for scout activities. They offered it to me for a big all-day outing I was planning as a scout leader. Before I left to get it, I added up what the cost of a couple of bows and arrows, a tug-of-war rope, some obstacle course equipment, flags, whistles, barrels, and lashing logs would be and it came to a couple hundred dollars. Since I sponsor activities of this type every so often, I gave my wife a check and told her just to buy the stuff on her next trip to town. She did. Five years and many "day camps" later, I figured up how much borrowing the equipment would have cost me, with the 100 miles (two trips back and forth each time) I'd have to drive plus my own time to do it, and it came to over $1200!

Dad's muttering that afternoon in the borrower's dust has saved me tens of thousands of dollars and thousands of hours of time. Borrowing has its place, maybe, once in a great while, but it always costs!

If it blows off the clothesline, it isn't going to stay under it

In the old days, between the house and the barn, there was always a clothesline—a place to dry the wash, more dependable and durable than any Maytag. You just hung your wares out, and mother nature took it from there with her own breeze settings, and later you could retrieve your clothes—not just dry but air-fresh and clean-smelling.

The downside of this seemingly simple energy-saving deal had to do with how you fastened the objects on there. If it wasn't "secure" and a stiff wind happened to come up, those clothes would come down. And they seldom remained where they fell, but rolled through dirt and snagged through stickers and ended up on a fence or the nearest bush, in much worse condition than they started the day.

Anchoring the items on the line was always a lesson in thoroughness. Two clothespins would hold a sheet, three would be better, and four would be sure. Did you hang two socks per pin or six or try for more? Gathering that tromped and muddy fallout from the ground or where it wrapped around a tree trunk, or chasing the dog playfully dragging your best pair of Levis around was a lesson I never forgot.

Likewise, in business, problems never stay in the same room or department where they happen. Anything that comes loose ripples through the rest of your operation and is seldom entirely fixed by correcting the source.

The clothesline taught that the most intelligent way to prevent problems is to hang your deals with "the baker's dozen"—an extra

clothespin, one or two more nails in the board or turns on the nut or screw, one or two extra tugs on the cinch, an extra wrap of the rope or look at the books. It costs almost nothing in time, yet it will keep your business in line as well as it keeps clothes on the line. One extra stamp on that important letter beats a three-day (or three-week!) delay for insufficient postage. Taking five or ten minutes for that confirming note or call will do a lot to prevent lost and forgotten deals and appointments. Extra clothespins are the cheapest part of doing business or wash.

Choice, not chance!

For years in youth I heard, "Farming is a gamble" and into maturity I heard, "Business is a gamble" (85 percent of new businesses fail). Good farmers convinced me to not buy into this appraisal. A good farmer or businessperson can always make choices; he never depends on or is limited by chance.

True, you can't control the frost, rain, wind, the economy, and many other plagues that often afflict farm and factory. However, good farmers and good businesspeople can prepare for and control their response to situations. They control selection and motivation of hired help, they control timing, spending and saving, working hours, and the focus of the farm or business. Knowing that mankind, animals, and the Earth have a history of some reverses, we aren't just victims of an outcome if we include such possibilities in our planning. Make hay when sun shines, and if it doesn't make whey, or something else another way. It's not gambling at all—just getting off your butt and adjusting.

Steers try

"Try" is a word that should be stricken from the business vocabulary. What does "try" really mean? Nothing!

>   *I'll try to be there...*

>   *I'll try to pay you...*

>   *I'll try to fly this plane...*

"Try" is a favorite cry of nonproducers. Too often confused with doing, trying—no matter how much effort goes into it—doesn't count.

You can go on the roundup, ride and rope, eat chuckwagon food, sing western songs, and wear out your saddle and Levis, but if you don't bring home any cows, it doesn't count. You can try to fix the engine, to cook, or to add to your collection, but if the engine doesn't run, no food appears on the table, or your butterfly net ends up empty, it doesn't count.

Try is such a lame, worthless word that if you use it around our office, you're fired. Where did I get such a firm opinion on such an unfirm word? You guessed it again, in the barnyard. Male cows destined for the meat locker were relieved of their reproductive capacities when young, and thereafter were "eunuchs on the hoof" that could not possibly breed. Yet even so you'd often see a steer assume a breeding position on a heifer in heat, hence the famous barnyard sarcasm, "Steers try."

Try is just an excuse word; it doesn't do the job. "Steer" clear of it.

If you feed the stock, they stay in the corral

Turnover is unquestionably one of the biggest headaches of modern business. When a good person quits or leaves, the ripples from it can pass through the whole chain of command, your entire operation. It can negatively affect a facility for years. Replacement (or "roundup") costs can be staggering and far from cost-effective. If you can't hold on to your people, crews, staff, team, you'll sink as a businessperson—fast.

We had the sure cure for this in the barnyard. "If you feed your stock, they stay in the corral" was the byword for proper care of the critters. It worked, too. Animals who are taken care of seldom stray. It's hungry animals that create havoc, rip up fences and ravage crops, break out and leave. Many times back on the ranch, a fence would get knocked down, or the main gate left open, but the cows, curious and greedy as they are, would still come back and stick around the stack. They could have cruised clear to Montana, but chose to only wander

a few hundred feet and then head back. Higher fences, more fervent curses, threats, contract binders, and pre-employment agreements don't keep either cows or people. Good care does! Put your money on that.

P. S. Some might make it to Montana, but will call to come home.

Don't start the roundup until the pen is ready

Here is the reality of getting the horse ahead of the cart. Catching the cow does you little good if you haven't made provision for securing it afterward. Bringing home the bacon is a wasted victory if there is nowhere to cook or keep it. Even good planning loses value if not done well ahead of the project. Many enterprising businessfolks gain an impressive acquisition only to end up without provision for it. They launched without a landing place, got the order or job but weren't prepared to deliver the goods. Barn wisdom says to have a spot ready for what you seek.

Fix it BEFORE it fails

We can all see what's sagging, cracking, rotting, or rusting, be it a gate, a pen, or our own personality or performance. When it finally fails, it's like getting fired—we have damage to deal with now instead of merely repair. Ready to break is not broken—no cows are out, but the opportunity for them to be out is at hand. Timely repair is always superior to recovery, and when some things (like relationships for example) fail they can never be fixed. Much easier to tighten the hinge now than to fish the door out of the manure after it falls off. An unhappy customer, like a leaning fence, can be straightened with a fraction of the effort and expense it will take if either topples. The less time you spend on problems, the more time you have to get things done.

Keep the path clear

Ninety-nine percent of livestock (or staff) will follow (stay in the bounds of) a clearly marked path. But if the path (like the company's goals or direction) gets weed-covered or otherwise unidentifiable, workers and livestock will wander all over the place, get lost, and destroy property. Well worn and marked trails get well used.

Fence sense

The ultimate Harvard Business School class would be Fencing 101. Fences on a farm, like rules and policies in business, were established to outline and regulate things. Fences keep both the animals and their owners safe and well, by keeping them in their own territory and marking the boundaries of ethics and expectations. Almost every principle of good fence management has a perfect parallel in business.

When to build

One of the first things the pioneer farmer did to establish a farm and homestead was fence the barn lot, a corral, then the house, then the fields around it and the border of the property. This helped establish not only domain, but purpose, job assignments, and function. The right time to build fences, at the homestead or in the home office, is right at the beginning.

Where to build

Get your "surveyors" to check it out first. If fences aren't built in the right place, there will be contention, disputes, and lawsuits.

Build the right kind of fence

You need to be sure that the subject or product can't go over, under, or through the barricade you are constructing. Rooting pigs, tiny baby chicks, and snorting two-ton buffalo, for instance, need different kinds of barriers.

Make them strong

Build them right the first time—trouble only begins when a fence fails. Any fence will be tested—wind and weather will buffet it, trees and branches will fall on it, and 1500-pound animals will rub on and try to reach through it. In business, employees and managers will lean on, reach through, and often try to breach your fences (policies). Anticipate this while building—you'll rarely hear any regrets about a fence built too strong.

The posts

These hold up the fence, keep it in place. Most wood posts will rot and break over time, for instance, if not treated, as will our

leaders (executives and other key personnel) if not treated right and strongly committed.

Fences project image

Tight, straight, freshly painted, weed-free fences and fencelines speak welcome, prosperity, and security, while a saggy fence conveys a sagging business.

Fences serve both sides

"Line" fences on the farm often have two owners because they have two purposes—to keep things in (contained) and to keep things out. Good fences require cooperation between neighbors (suppliers and clients or customers).

Maintenance is a must

Riding fence (see page 60) is an important part of management, so that weak, damaged, or broken places can be fixed before the cows (customers) get out or the wolves get in.

Fences need gates

There are times when we need to cut through fences (and formalities) quickly and efficiently, times when we need quick access to the other side, both coming and going. Easy, well-oiled gates say, "welcome," and relieve pressure on fences.

Old fences need to be removed

Once a fence (policy or boundary) is no longer useful, it needs to be torn down or carefully disassembled. And all of its remains (old rusty wire, broken posts, etc.) removed!

The electric fence

For those of you who have never been jolted by one, an electric fence consists of an innocent-looking strand or two of electrified wire held up by small metal stakes. It's a simple, inexpensive way to keep animals under control. Once they know they'll get a shock if they lean or touch against it, they won't go near it. An electric fence gets its current from a small metal box generally hung in the barn.

Those of us who grew up with electric fences kept our distance, but still, every once in a while, we'd be standing in an irrigation puddle and happen to touch the fence with a wet shovel handle and *wham*, we knew it. Crawling under one and raising yourself up too soon would also keep you current. You only fooled your city slicker cousins with an electric fence once, and sporty boys peeing on it never repeated the act.

All in all, electric fences were a positive. They saved time, fencing expenses, and animals' lives, and intelligent use of an electric fence did a good job of keeping stock in place. Yet many of our neighbors were forever fighting stock that got out, even with the fence on high. Their animals would walk up to the wire or try to jump it—get shocked doing it, and then bolt the rest of the way out. A thin wire or two, after all, isn't nearly as intimidating to a 2,000-pound animal as a sturdy five-foot fence.

But that flimsy electric fence will hold animals perfectly if you just prepare them for it. For a couple of weeks at the end of the winter, just before turning the stock out to pasture, Dad would stretch an electric wire (with the current on low) across one end of the corral, and toss some hay behind it. The cows or horses or whatever would come sniffing, licking, and testing, up to the fence and get a buzz, a couple of little surprises, and after that they all knew what the wire was and respected it. Once they were actually out in the field, they weren't interested in the bad experience of trying to get through it.

I guess the fence taught me the principle of spelling out boundaries and then making sure your people understand them. This saves the unpleasantries of rounding them up or fixing the broken hearts or broken contracts afterward. Sometimes on the farm the fence would be off for weeks and the cows would still never wander, because they knew the rules. We all set up "electric fences" (boundaries) when we

set up business. Make sure people know what, where, and why they are—don't wait till they're in the field, right up against them, to test them.

P. S. Any tall grass stalks or weeds that were allowed to touch the fence would short it out and steal the electricity; so the wire had to be clean and clear to function well. That tells us something about boundaries, too.

Riding fence

We had some "stand-around jobs" on the ranch—things to do when and if everything else was done and caught up. If nothing much was happening right then, instead of hanging and loafing around, you did a stand-around job. The very first one on the list always was: ride fence.

Fences don't stay strong on their own. The snow sags and strains them, big heavy animals lean on them, sun and rain rot them, lazy hunters cut them, and weeds and bushes and trees grow into and through them. If you just put up a fence and forget about it, there will always come an emergency—**the stock is out!** Once the stock is out, you can count on trouble: Crops will be destroyed, animals eat so much they get bloated, some will run off and be lost or injured or stolen, and others will trample the neighbors' lawns and graze on the neighbors' prize flowers. A broken fence is sure to mean broken friendships or relationships.

Smart people don't wait for fences to break before giving them attention. In my company we call this preventive maintenance; back when I was a boy it was "riding fence." We'd set out with a tractor and some tools and wire and follow the fencelines, tightening the wire where it was sprung, adding a few staples, replacing any broken or rotten posts, cleaning out any growth that threatened the wire, etc. It was always a fast and minor job; it only took a few hours. But it kept us from losing days on roundup and replacement because "the fence was down."

Any day is a good day to fix fences.

That big difference between gross and net

When I was a teenager, we lived on a ranch surrounded by eighty miles of desert. My brothers and I worked for my father and individual profitmaking opportunities out there seemed as remote as where we lived. Then, when I was thirteen, I heard on the radio that the Kasper Keck Hide and Tallow Yard was paying five dollars a ton for prairie bones. Gads! I had fenced and herded on the range for years and seen the bleached bones of expired livestock all over the place. I'd also driven teams of horses and milked cows, had them tromp on my toes, and so I knew, as Dad said, "Some of them weigh near a ton." I was pretty excited about the profits just lying out there on the prairie to be plucked.

So on foot, with a burlap "gunny sack," I scoured the face of many acres in my time off. All those big old bones rubbed blisters on my back as I carried sack after sack home and stored them in a pile against the granary—just like stacking gold in reserve! Finally, I could subdue the urge to "cash in" no longer. We hauled them all to old Kasper, to be converted to calcium for fertilizer. Dad brought a check home... for $3.72! (for 1352 pounds). Samson, who slew a thousand Philistines with the jawbone of an ass, could appreciate how I felt after picking up what seemed like a thousand jawbones and feeling like their former owner!

There is a BIG difference between gross and net, another early farm lesson. It's easy to forget—or lose sight of the fact—that what you make is only what is left after subtracting *all* of your expenses.

Professor barn cat (MBA, PhD)

Many people think I don't like cats because, having been raised on a farm, I think that having a cat in the house is about the same as having a horse or cow in there. All the house cats I know are lazy, spoiled, surly, ungrateful, and expensive, but a barn cat, now there is an animal worth observing, especially for anyone who wants to succeed in business.

A barn cat is beautiful. It may pick up a few thistles and burrs, but its coat is usually thick and gleaming. It has long, sharp claws and moves like a well-oiled bearing. Best of all it is totally self-supporting and productive. You never see a barn cat slithering and meowing up to a food dish, checking out the perks and bonuses. They live free, frugal, and full of fire.

All you young businesspeople should come out for a day with your legal pads and notebooks and observe how one of these models of modern ethics operates. You'll be tough to beat on the business floor if you imitate some of their virtues. What would you learn if you watched? Barn cats are:

Quick:

People are pretty slow and lethargic in business anymore—no one leaps, runs, or hustles. Everyone is balancing coffee and a snack and being oh-so-careful of their clothes and image. They take hours, days, weeks to respond to an assignment or request, even something that could be done in minutes. Barn cats get the job done quickly because they move! When they go after something it isn't with an old house cat amble; they strike like a rattlesnake or lightning. Their quickness is delightful and refreshing to see, and their prey (clients) seldom escape.

Patient:

Fast as they might move in battle, when they are planning and strategizing they're quiet and focused. And they have the patience to wait for the perfect moment.

Prompt:

Barn cats are on the job at 5 A.M., a good time for any getter-doner to get up and get on with it.

Dependable:

If a mouse or rat is lurking around eating things up and pooping on things, you just let the cat in and on the job and you don't have to worry about it anymore. How many of us can you say that about? It can be forty below or a 110 degrees in the shade, and the barn cat is still out and about, checking up on things. You can be fighting your way from the house to the barn after the biggest snowfall of the decade, and there ahead of you are the barn cat's tracks. It would be hard to find a better example of energy and industry.

Brave:

There are some real scaredy cats in business anymore: wimping around in job-protecting poses, sulking around, afraid to ever speak up or move in case they might possibly displease or upset someone in a high position. Cowards are a real disgrace to our ranks, concentrating in their piddly political arenas on designing and redesigning forms, or who has the biggest desk or most elegant office. They have no guts to go for what they really want or should do or say.

If you watch and follow the barn cats going about their business you'll see polite, but imposing predators. They aren't aggressive or pushy but will venture under the heaviest hoof with no fear of getting tromped. They'll climb to the highest, most precarious place and around deadly electric wires to nail fair game. When VP (Vicious Pup) or the biggest hound dog invades their food or territory, they don't pussyfoot around in political diplomacy. They rip right into someone even ten times their size, and usually send them bleeding and yelping back to the boss.

Self-reliant:

The business world is overflowing now with perk hunters and guarantee seekers; insecure, overeducated folks whose first and major concern about a firm is will it assure them a secure future (as a general job benefit, mind you, not merely something you earn by merit). No self-respecting barn cat would sell its soul for a golden parachute that must be procured before the employee in question has ever produced anything. Barn cats don't ask for free housing, or two months off to have kittens—they hunt and serve right up to the day before and will be back on the job the same day of any wound or weather reverse.

Grateful:

One of the greatest weaknesses of today's businesspeople is ungratefulness. Too many employees, because they attended a few years of school, think they are fully qualified and deserving of being taken care of in every way by their employer. Or because they have designer stationery and a BMW, they think the public should automatically pay attention to them. Every one of us in business should spend a few minutes in meditation each week, in thanksgiving for the very privi-

lege and freedom of being allowed to get out there and compete. We see so many people who are overpaid and underworked, and plenty, too, who may be industrious and productive, but are also haughty and arrogant and totally ungrateful for the position, income, and opportunities for self-development they have.

I'll never forget how barn cats, on the other hand, after working their paws to the bone to keep the barnyard pest-free, would line up quietly by the stanchion when we did the morning and evening milking. They never begged or yowled, just bowed their heads humbly suggesting that maybe a squirt of warm milk would be appreciated. So from eight or ten feet away with perfect aim I'd shoot a stream of milk into their mouths, and when I quit, full or not they wouldn't whine or pout, just lick their lips and nod a thanks and get back to work.

Bigger isn't necessarily better

The herds on our ranch were from 25 to 120 head, so you can imagine my awe when I visited a feedlot of over 10,000 critters with my dad. More than the sheer mass of cattle, I remember the owner of all those cows. He seemed like a nice, sincere man but as he talked and led us from pen to pen, I couldn't help noticing the holes in his socks. Grandma always said that even a poor man can have good socks, and here this fellow who owned all these thousands and thousands of cows had big ugly holes in his socks. Every time he put his feet up on the corral they flashed like a neon sign to me.

Riding home I asked Dad why a man rich enough to have a hundred times as many cows as us and all our neighbors put together would have holey socks. These may not be the exact words, but in summary he said: It's not how much stock you handle and have around, it's how much you keep after they're sold. I drove by that huge barnyard a couple of years later and it was empty, deserted, not one single cow. Dad with our hundred head made more profit than the big rancher with 10,000. That was a clear message I never forgot.

Thinking along the lines of "Gee, we're making a good living milking 40 cows, let's milk 80 and double it" is usually oversimplified. It seldom happens without plenty of extra effort and unforeseen new expenses. Most farm failures are people who were doing well and went after bigger and got buried. Most of the biggest struggles, most murderous pressure, and worst setbacks in business come in the process of going for more.

Bigger may mean more volume, and more attention, maybe, but more profit and satisfaction don't automatically follow. All of us starting up a business are initially thankful to survive and eat, but before long that prompting to be BIG creeps in. How big you are is always the first thing job seekers and the media want to hear about. Size has a fascination and it's a dangerous one. Yes, expansion, improvement, and growth are important to a business, but that doesn't necessarily mean being big. How about "better?" If you're better long enough you can become big without trying. Whenever I find myself getting in the "big" lane in my travels or transactions, I remember the man with the holey socks, and switch back to the better or best road.

All soils aren't the same!

"Dirt is dirt and people are people."

You'll live pretty sparsely, if not poorly, if you believe and practice that!

Even on the very same farm, there can be a half-dozen or more different soil types. No matter what field you work in, the soil will be different—sometimes a little, sometimes a lot. Some soils are loose and airy; others heavy and easily packed down. Some hold water forever and others lose it quickly. Some can be plowed early or only late. Some will grow great carrots and potatoes and others only knobby blobs. As soon as you get to know a soil, you'll lessen your toil and improve your harvest.

I remember as a little kid the county agent coming to our farm to do "soil surveys." He went field to field taking soil samples in little glass tubes and then tested them, and came back and told Dad that this field was lacking something, while another not far away had too much of something else. Dad did some adjustments with lime and fertilizer and rotated crops to compensate, and some of the yields were almost a third higher.

Likewise, in business, you can't treat all people, customers, negotiations, or sales the same. When you set foot on new or even old ground here, stop and take a sample of the customer or the commodity you're working with. Maybe by adding just a touch of this or holding back on that, you'll start increasing your harvest.

Straighten your rows at the first sign of sag

There is an unwritten rule of straightness in rural life—not letting rows or fences, stacks or windrows, ditches or corral gates bend or bow, even a little. Learning how to "sight in" for a straight anything came right after the ABCs for a real farm person, if you wanted to keep any dignity.

Dad's and Grandpa's rows and fences were straight as arrows, but as soon as they let me take over mine would immediately begin to weave, twist, and tail off. And each time I'd follow the slightly crooked one I'd just caused, so the next one was even more erratic or as Dad so bluntly put it, "Good grief, Donald, it looks like a snake" (and it did). I managed to live to age sixteen to see the day my rows, fences, and gates were equal to theirs and to this day I've never figured out why they didn't teach me how to go straight, before they laughed at my "S" curve installations.

In case you missed out too or have forgotten (or unfortunately missed a rural raising), there are two rules for staying straight:

1. Pick a point far away at the end of the row, sight in on it, and key all your movements to it precisely, never looking down to the side marker or behind you.

2. If you do happen to slip, stagger, or lurch in your precision pursuit, or make a boo-boo, correct it to that original point you picked right on the very next row. Get back on course immediately—don't let the bulge build and try to correct it gradually.

This "straight sense" from the farm field is a lifesaver in business. We set courses, rules, standards, quotas, etc., daily. When some slippage, relaxation, or deviation occurs or we drift off course, most of us follow the drift while trying to correct our course and end up so far off we find ourselves operating crooked as a snake. Fix your eye on the final goal and *straighten your course at the first sign of sag*—not after you've lost your way.

There's no easy relief in a runaway

You don't have to be in business long to learn that something out of control can put you out of business in days, hours, even minutes. Some companies have full-time "troubleshooters" or "problem solvers," which I'd be ashamed to admit to—the way to handle trouble is to *prevent* it. No matter how quickly or brilliantly you solve a problem, when you get done, you're right where you were when you started. So basically you've accomplished nothing.

Business executives like to say in a deep voice of wisdom, "We can handle a few survivable mistakes." What is a survivable mistake? Most mistakes are survivable. Our goal should be eliminating problems, not learning how to handle them more efficiently.

Once your business gets out of control, it's no simple matter to regain it. You don't control out of control things—you're at their mercy. Just let something go and you'll see what I mean.

I remember back on the ranch once we had a cracked tongue on one of the wagons. In case you've never seen one, a tongue is the sturdy wooden beam that runs from the front of a wagon up between the horses, and keeps the wagon from running into the team when you're going downhill. We knew that weakened tongue was trouble waiting to happen, but figured we could make it through haying season. One nice mild morning, having just emptied the wagon, my brother and I were headed home. Going down a hill, the weight of the wagon started pushing the horses. I pulled on the reins to hold them back, and the strain was just enough to snap the tongue. With nothing holding it back now, the wagon smacked the team right on the rump and they lunged. I managed to hold them for a minute, but the wagon had enough momentum to whack them even harder now and that was it.

One of the horses lurched, then kicked and splintered the front of the wagon, and the team bolted. "Runaway"—it looks so adventurous in the movies, but in real life it's just pure terror—a horse can run like a racecar when it's scared. Our team swerved off the paved road and thundered down toward the gravel pit, and we were moving so fast that every time we hit a bump or ditch the wagon flew five or six feet into the air. We couldn't jump off because there was a fierce fence on

one side and a busy highway on the other. It would just be suicide. Besides, if we did manage to abandon the spooked team, Dad would probably do worse things to us than our landing did.

The reins led to bits in the tender mouths of the horses, and I handed my brother one of the reins, and took the other. We braced our feet against what was left of the front of the wagon and pulled with all our two-hundred-plus pounds of pressure. We didn't even faze them; they were so wild we passed our neighbor, in his new pickup, in a cloud of dust. By now we were thoroughly terrified, and the runaways seemed determined not to stop till we hit the next canal, which would be something like Evel Knievel's leap over the Snake River. Fortunately, real horses (unlike those amazing movie horses) can only run at a pace like that for a few miles, so eventually they did slow down, and as we approached Canal Hill, they stopped.

That was my last runaway and a lesson learned: Use your energy to fix the weak parts of your business, instead of struggling to get control of a runaway!

If they know home, they won't leave home

Both businesses and barnyards get new blood from the outside from time to time. A new face around the corral or conference room means you better do some orientation. If you merely acquire a new staff or herd member and turn him or her loose (in the pasture or on the job) and leave, as too many bosses and farmers do, there's at least an 80 percent likelihood that things will go bad.

Back home on the ranch, when we were introducing a new critter, we always made a point of keeping it confined in close quarters for a while, so it could get acclimated to its new master and the sights, sounds, and smells of its new home. Otherwise the newcomer would be hit by homesickness, and that was where it would head, be it one mile or twenty. Animals could make a beeline back to where they came from in hours, and it was pretty embarrassing to show up at the seller's house with an empty trailer, asking for the critter you just bought.

Because we all feel at home already where we are, when we bring a new person to the office or crew we often forget this. So we get a similar runaway situation, called turnover. Modern, scientific hiring statistics support the old barnyard principle: If you make newcomers feel at home and give them time to settle in, they're much more likely to stick around.

"Root, hog, or die!"

The first time I heard this phrase, it was from an uncle who said it at the table right after the blessing on the food. The minute the platters hit the tablecloth he announced enthusiastically, "All right, dig in! Around here it's root, hog, or die!" I had no idea what that meant, even when everyone at the table grabbed, reached, chomped, and gobbled fiercely.

A few years later, after choosing hogs as my FFA project, the translation of my uncle's battle cry was clear. Soon I had 72 tiny hyper pigs I fed separated milk to in a trough that accommodated only 62. "Root, hog, or die" was self-explanatory—pigs are by nature enthusiastic and hungry and whoever got to the trough fastest and managed to stay in place profited. The others, the latecomers, were wedged and crowded out and they just oinked around staring at pig butts, listening to slurps!

Likewise, I've found that some real secrets of business success are:

1. Being enthused and hungry.
2. Knowing what and where the trough is.
3. Getting there first and holding firmest.

It's truly the process of root, hog, or die!

Know where your pitchforks are!

When Charlie Chaplain or the Three Stooges were anywhere near a haystack, they'd always end up sitting on a pitchfork and yeooowing. In business or the barnyard, you always want to know where your pitchforks are, and not only to keep from being stuck. The pitchfork is a key tool of the barnyard; it tosses the hay in and the reprocessed hay (manure) out. It looks a little like a table fork, and it's just as important to the nourishment of the barnyard. If you fail to know where your pitchforks are, you pay a big price. Leaving one down somewhere almost guarantees it will be stepped on by a 2,000-pound animal and broken, or buried under the snow, run over, pooped on, or otherwise violated by the weather or traffic, animal or mechanical. And you can be sure that when you show up to service the barnyard, you won't be able to find it. Have you ever tried to serve hay or remove soggy bedding with just your bare hands, or tested your tender heel against the tines of a razor-sharp fork? In either case, you lose!

Back on the ranch we learned this lesson quickly. The pitchfork was our lifeline, and we took care of it. In business we have employees that are as important as the farmer's pitchfork—they're our lifeline to our customers, our means of feeding them and caring for them, keeping them happy and comfortable. We need to care for them exactly the same way. If we toss them around and neglect them, they too will get stepped on, pooped on, broken, rusted, and covered with cold treatment. Then suddenly we're groping around some morning, or in an urgent moment of business need, unable to find them and unable to do what we need to without them.

The rule of the barnyard was, before you go into the house to rest or before you leave the area, carefully stick your fork in a high, protected place where wind, rain, snow, or stock can't get to it. Treat your pitchforks well and they'll do more than give you a hand, they will be your hands.

Spud secrets

Living in Idaho as I did as a child, picking potatoes offered a season of opportunity which I capitalized on. In potato season they let school out for two weeks. Once I'd done the work Dad gave me, I could pick spuds for the neighbors. In four years of picking, my partner (my hard-working sister Shirley) and I never came in second to anyone. When we reached the fields and I'd yell out, "We can outpick anyone!" My sister would tell me to shut my big mouth, and then we would work like demons to win.

We left the wimps in the dust, but there were always some older kids and grownups who kept up with us, even a little ahead of us. By about three or four o'clock in the afternoon, which was often the hottest part of the day, they would buckle or need a break and we'd surge ahead.

Picking 350 sacks (most others did around 200) at seven cents a sack, meant at least

$12.25 earned apiece a day, and that was big money. An awesome 400-sack day was a staggering $14 each. At the end of spud season we often had more than a hundred dollars tucked away, which took care of Christmas, school expenses, a piece or two of athletic gear, and even a few ice cream sundaes. I loved picking spuds; loved competing.

We had the #1 reputation with all the farmers and always had plenty of job offers. We were first in the field in the morning and last to leave at night. There was something about the combination of winning and earning that kept one from ever getting tired!

I learned two big principles of success here—that working long hours and working fast gave you more than average.

Going broke on breaks

I was putting on one of my first business seminars, for thirty executives assembled in a swanky meeting room. I started at 8 A.M. promptly, and true to my raving lunatic style of presenting, ripped into the subject with visuals and facts that created audible gasps and applause. I usually teach with an intensity that doesn't lose audiences, but at about 9:30 A.M. I noticed nervous glances at wristwatches, squirming, eye-rolling, leg-crossing, and other strange movements in the group. So I cranked my speed up another notch and laid it on thicker and faster. By ten o'clock the whole room seemed in twitching turmoil and finally a big burly guy in the back leaped to his feet and yelled, "Let us go!" "Go where?" I asked. "To the bathroom," came the chorus back.

I said, "Well, okay," and dismissed them for five minutes, and no stampede of alarmed cattle could have equaled the surge through that door to the restrooms.

In the middle of the afternoon session, 1-5 P.M., I sensed another uprising brewing and asked, "Do you people have to go again?" They erupted like the Tabernacle Choir on the last hallelujah verse.

At the end of the day, the head guys called me aside and explained the birds and bees of breaks in their company. "Breaks?" I asked. "We aren't working, just sitting." I'd never heard of a "break," and not being a coffee drinker or one who stayed up half the night boozing, I didn't have a clue that people often used the bathroom several times a day!

Back on the farm a working day had only three events: starting time, noon, and quitting time. On the farm we got up at 5 A.M., milked the cows, ate at 6 A.M., went to the bathroom once, and that was it

until noon. Quitting time was when the job was done, not when our strength gave out.

Lunch too had a perspective on the ranch that could help us all have a more profitable business. "Power lunches," "Out to lunch," "Can I buy you lunch?" "He isn't back from lunch yet," are things we hear often in business, all meaning a big interruption in a productive day. Sure we do have to eat, however we don't always have to make a big ceremony out of a little nourishment. The amount of time and money spent to "lunch" these days is often considerable. Lunch is for sustenance, and sometimes for negotiation, discussion, or getting acquainted, not for a mini-vacation from work. We learned on the farm that when machinery was in operation, stock moving, or work flowing, that bringing it to a halt to leave and eat was often a real drawback and stride-breaker. At noon we often ate in the field, sometimes not even turning the tractor motor off (too hard to restart). Having a quick bite at the job site saved daylight and kept production going. Losing an hour or more just to take in some food and a drink wasn't necessary.

There's a lot to be said for returning to the farm concept of lunch, a brief bite at work, leaving culinary adventures and explorations for the end of the day, or a big breakfast before the day. Skipping lunch might even make sense sometimes (and even be healthy these days in our overweight society).

Don't stop walking just because you're wounded

"I don't feel good" was a sick statement to make around the barnyard, "SO? Go out and announce that to the stock or the crops, do you think they care? Should the animals starve or the silage spoil just because you ache?"

There was no sick leave on the farm. How one felt was irrelevant if something needed to be done. Who could call in sick when the irrigation water needed to be turned on, the cows milked, or babies fed? If you had an ailment anywhere from strep throat to a smashed hand, you didn't stay home in bed or run to the doctor, you bandaged yourself up and went to work. This seemed brutal to me at the time; now I know it was a training everyone should have before they get a business license. In business we get so many wounds and afflictions, whether we deserve them or not. Unjust lawsuits are slapped on us, we get "cut" by financial losses, stabbed by competitors, our hearts are broken by disappointments, and our backs strained with overload. The business world will regularly wound anyone involved in it, and you can't just lie down and die or retreat to the sickbed. Only the weak and uncommitted let themselves succumb like that.

Any wound—physical, emotional, or financial—can drain the "want to" right out of our body and spirit, but it never eliminates the "have to." Just because you're hurting, you don't quit working. Discomfort isn't a reason to dodge responsibilities. Would John Wayne ever have tossed down his gun because he got wounded?

Persistence and endurance don't develop in character that winds down when the wounds come, and without persistence and endurance you'll never make much of a mark in business or life. Blood at the barnyard meant a Band Aid or big bandage, not beating a trail to time off, or giving up. You didn't take off to return when healed up—you walked while wounded, and you healed while you walked. Hurt didn't mean helpless.

I remember well when at the age of thirteen I was promoted to hay stacker, which meant I got to do a grown man's job up on the stack. As a load (about 1000 pounds of hay) was lifted up from the ground and dumped on top of the stack, I would pitch it around to the edges, etc., to shape the stack straight and tall. It was the hottest, ugliest job imaginable, plus with the hay often came rocks, rattlesnakes, wire, and weeds with sharp prickles. It was no picnic, but knowing I was the key member of the crew kept me going. I *had* to keep stacking or everything stopped.

One day, when I was stacking, a load had already been dropped in place on our now 20-foot high stack, and it took me only a few minutes to manage it, so standing a foot deep in the hay I decided to catch my breath. I wanted to rest leaning on the pitchfork, so I jabbed it down hard in the hay, not stopping to think that my foot was down there too. That sharp, glistening, pencil-sized tine went right through the middle of my foot. Alarmed, I yelled down, "Dad, I've stuck the fork through my foot!" Dad yelled back up, "Well pull it out—there's another load coming up!"

I did, and quickly, a hurt foot being not nearly as bad as being buried by a giant load of hay. These days Dad would probably be run in for child abuse, but the attitude I learned there toward responsibility has blessed my life. Many a night that I've come home totally discouraged, and many a morning, beginning a day I'd much rather not, I take off my shoes and socks and see that round scar on top of my

foot. And suddenly my heart is lightened and I chuckle. It was a great wound—I couldn't clean homes without it.

If you're on your back long enough, you'll drown

A neighbor of ours once had a cow that drowned in a ditch it could easily have jumped over or walked right out of. The problem was, it had slipped somehow so that it was on its back. When I asked Grandpa how such a big animal could drown in such a little bit of water, he said, "No matter how good a swimmer you are, if you're on your back long enough, you'll drown."

How true this really was only came home to me as I waded into the business world and found myself and my fellow businesspeople all getting into "ditches," too. We'd slip or slide or even walk right into them, but poor judgment of some kind was usually involved. We'd get in debt or into a quagmire like a partly useful but really unsatisfactory employee. Instead of struggling to our feet, calling for help, or otherwise taking care of the situation, we just keep twitching and thrashing and gasping for air. If we keep it up we'll drown—go bankrupt, or sell out.

Next time you find yourself in a ditch, lie still a minute, think the problem over, and then whinny for help or make one good lunge upward or otherwise get out *immediately*. The longer you lay there and thrash and struggle the deeper you'll sink and weaker you'll get. And "drowning" (failure) is no fun for you or your family or clients.

Don't park in the middle of a moving herd

Once in a while in the game of business, as in a basketball game, there is something called a fast break. Everyone is down by the home team basket and suddenly some opportunist intercepts a pass and heads for the other end. At a moment like this you can't steal or work a play to get to the other end, you just have to run like crazy, sprinting and yelling to get in on the action before they score.

When a business market is hot, a lot is going on, everyone is moving and doing. Energy is high and people are spirited and motivated. This is always the time to quicken your pace, to forget to rest, to burn the candle, to move with and for the world of business.

Too many of us, instead, just park ourselves in the middle of some great goings-on with the idea that somehow some of it will rub off on us. Somehow we'll absorb some of the fallout and activity and prosper. It just doesn't work that way—you've got to move with the herd and rub noses and shoulders with them. You've got to negotiate positions and peddle your wares. Just parking in the middle of the action won't do it.

I saw a perfect example of this one day in a barnyard. Some townie drove his fancy pickup and horse trailer out into the middle of a pasture and just left it there while he went off to do something else. It was a sharp outfit—lots of clean, shiny chrome, special ornaments, antennas, all kinds of bells and whistles. Obviously he didn't understand cattle and horses. Anything that's still, stationary, they'll go and rub themselves on. In just a few hours, when the fellow returned, both of the side view mirrors were off on the ground, several pieces of chrome had been relocated, and there was animal hair stuck in the crevices of all of the rest of it. One of the antennas was bent (from horse neck scratching), and they had chewed on his vehicle, scraped it, licked it and slobbered on it, and in general done an unbelievable amount of damage.

I left a big tough old tractor out in the barnyard overnight once, and even that seemingly impossible to hurt thing was worked over and damage done to the paint job, lights, and wiring. When you're in motion animals will leave you and your conveyance alone; park somewhere and you are an instant scratching post.

When there is action, don't be parked somewhere in a chair—*move*.

If you work in the herd, you're going to get stepped on!

So don't whine about it, just limp quietly! Heavy traffic always generates heavy abuse… there is more crowding, milling, squeezing, shoving, stumbling, complaining, cheating, and biting in the thick than in the thin of it. If those seeking a business career can learn just this single thing, they will be in a position to select (not just accept, after it's too late) the climate they want to work in.

Herds on the ranch were the best parallel to the "rat race." Working in herds you have to move fast to stay alive, and you take getting pooped on and bellowed at for granted. If stampedes, or getting tromped on a few times a day scares you, stay with a small herd or no

herd—work in a small corral somewhere, not the main ranch. In the big herd pressure is part of the package.

Take it down before it falls down

On the farm, just like other businesses, we built things to store, support, house, cover, hold, carry, sell, or host projects and demands. Thus we had corrals, chutes, barns, bridges, gates, fences, windbreaks, mangers, and pens, among others. Some of these structures were used for a season and some longer, but many eventually outgrew their function and purpose. Or they simply wore down and out from weather or crop and livestock use. Far too many farm folks just left them there then to make a kind of barnyard ghost town, waiting for the elements to blend them back into the soil. Most of these things refused to die standing, so they leaned about forever in dismemberment and disgrace. Or for the next owner to worry about, tear down, and clean up.

Nothing does less for efficiency or image than a bunch of old sheds or fences about; in the way physically and mentally. Junk buildings aren't just a safety and fire hazard, they provide prime housing for pests and always collect a bunch of broken-down smaller junk inside.

We didn't allow any shabby shanties or outmoded outbuildings on our place—and a good business of any kind should follow that law. Otherwise not only buildings, but obsolete tools or equipment, junk vehicles, no longer needed scaffolding, and "temporary" structures of any kind seem to hang around in the shade or shadow of the new forever.

> Anything left to fall into ruin is not just an eyesore but an eye opener: An all-too-clear indication that the owners are uncaring and not in full control of their property, hence their business. Once something's work is done, remove it from your premises and your balance sheet. You'll have a lot more room and send better signals to clients and customers, family and friends.

Go with your gut reactions

Some of the best advice I've ever heard, for business or for life is: "It pays to act on your first feeling or instinct." We all know those feelings well—a basic impulse to run, fight, quit, cry, or check something out registers in our brain well before any consideration of what's legal, logical, or political. It's amazing how bright and right our instincts often are. Animals have them in a far more refined form, but we do have them, and when and if we use them we'll often get far better results than by relying on any of the mere theories or social patterns we've learned.

You'll find that most of the really good, dynamic, brave businesspeople out there depend on instinct. True, they do read the postmortems and reports in *Inc., The Wall Street Journal*, etc., but deep inside they know that tapping the inner intelligence, the "gut feeling" of a live person makes a lot more sense in live business.

But is there a "better" way?

Having grown up in the seat of a Massey-Ferguson (the Lexus of tractors at the time), with wonderful hydraulics and overdrive, I quickly classed the ancient green John Deere "A" parked on a hill of the property I'd just bought as "junk." When I mentioned to our neighbor George Andrews that I was going to haul it off to the landfill, I found out that John Deere isn't just a tractor, it's a cult. He shook as if I'd taken a pitchfork to him, and then I got a thirty-minute testimonial on the merits of that old tractor. By the time he finished, that ancient

machine was sacred to me too. I committed to keeping it, and asked how to start it. On the left side was a heavy twenty-four-inch flywheel, which had a notch where a small hand crank could be inserted.

I cranked that stupid thing for thirty minutes, and was ready to quit when it finally gave a little "putt," which meant "Crank on, you moron, and I might just start!" Finally it did start—"putt-putt, putt-putt." I said, "Gadfreys, George, it's only hitting on two cylinders." "That's all it's got," he said. Well, once mounted up on it, pulling my old trusty scraper, I had to admit that baby pulled in a way my little Massey-Ferguson couldn't comprehend. I loved that big ugly old machine, but what a fight it was to start. I'd crank and crank and it would kick and sprain my thumb. At noon I'd pull it up by the kitchen and let it run while I wolfed down my dinner, so I wouldn't have to restart it.

This went on for about six months, until Thanksgiving morning. A light snow had fallen and a neighbor had slid off the road near our house. There was a knock on our door—"Mr. Aslett, would you mind pulling us out of the barrow pit with your tractor?" "Sure!" I jumped up on the back hitch to brush the snow off the tractor seat, and a small wire with a finger loop on the end just behind the hand clutch caught my eye. I'd seen it before, but I figured it was someone's little temporary repair. This time I reached down and pulled it, and "arrn, arrn, arrn, putt-putt, putt-putt," went the tractor. It had a starter all the time that I'd been cranking away at it like old George showed me. I'd still have been cranking today if I hadn't pulled that little wire!

Moral: One way, even though it works, is often not the only or even the best way. And how many of us in business have a starter we've never engaged?

Late costs

This is one of those lessons in business or on the farm that seems to take quite a few repeats before it really penetrates our noggin. It seems that nothing that needs to be done ever exactly fits our mood or inclination; we're never in a perfectly convenient location or situation to do it. But there are all kinds of things that call for precision timing in the barnyard, things that if you wait until you get around to it, you pay a high price for. If you milk at random hours, production will go down, your cows will get sore teats, and they'll come to the fence and moo their heads off. Or they'll show up at the barn at the appointed hour, wait a little while, and then leave—and then you'll have to round them up. If you wait a week to doctor an animal, the infection will be much worse or it may even be too late. Waiting till later, too, to fix fences, switch pastures, shorten horns, catch that predator, find that leak, haul manure, or chop feed will double or triple your work or mean "too late" when you finally do get to it. *On time* has to be one of the most critical aspects of any business operation. "Late" says to your customers, your boss, or the owner, in ten-foot-high letters:

I CAN'T HANDLE IT

I DON'T HAVE TIME ENOUGH

I JUST DON'T CARE ENOUGH

These are all bad things to say to the boss.

What has to be done has to be done. It'll take as much (or more) time later, and gain two tons of irritation in the meantime. "Later" is one of the biggest saboteurs of success in business. The unwillingness to put in extra hours when you need to, to be sure something is on time, when it was pledged or promised, is a big reason for business failure. Most successful businesspeople aren't any smarter or more talented; they don't have any better breaks or more luck. They just put in more hours on the job. This is a powerful secret few who moan about recessions and business setbacks have learned.

> Spend a month on a farm sometime, and keep the habits you learn. You'll be amazed to discover that life begins at 5 A.M., and you don't need the radio or a cup of coffee to get you going, either. Fresh air and the exhilaration of brisk motion does it all.

Some hangouts that don't help

There are places in life and business that are actually specifically designed to be idle. On the farm, for example, there was "the loafing shed" and just about every barnyard had one. It was usually just a lean-to type structure that provided a roof and some shade. It was a

place where animals hung out and did nothing but sleep, loaf, chew their cud, belch, swish away flies, and butt each other around a little. You might actually call it a livestock lounge, a place where they could pass some time and loiter life away.

We humans have plenty of our own "loafing sheds," called lounges, break rooms, recreation rooms, hospitality suites, student unions, fraternities, sororities, fraternal lodges, bowling alleys, and bars, among other things. In my early years after college, I found that even the school-teaching industry had a loafing shed, called the teachers' lounge. All of these are places where people, like cattle, can meet to dawdle and drone away long enough to dull any edge or ambition they might have brought to work with them.

In more than forty-five years in business I've stayed out of lounges of all kinds and it's given me a great advantage. It would be hard to total up all the extra things I've accomplished and excitement I've experienced while out in the world *doing* rather than sitting behind lounge doors loafing, all these years. No real businessperson has time for loafing sheds, and flies won't light on anyone who's moving. Imagine how you'd feel when the long-awaited moment to discuss your

raise or promotion comes, or a time when the boss really needs you, and when he or she asks where you are, "down in the loafing shed" (lounge) is the answer. Any image of loafing or lounging in business is negative and damaging.

Loafing sheds have a dead, dismal, do-nothing spirit that doesn't belong in business. The cattle and pigs at least digest their food and gain weight while "loafing," but maximum weight on sale day isn't our goal. Work is where we come to produce and do, to be moved and motivated!

Spurs make a good horse buck

Dad always made it clear that a good rider doesn't need or ever use spurs. "You don't have to gouge a good horse to make them run harder or mind." That was his and all my uncles' and grandparents' philosophy. Business is full of sad supervisors and managers who try to use spurs to up production and get respect. "Riders" use spurs; real horsemen use a pat on the neck. Remember, any injuries you inflict on those who work to help you achieve your goals will only make them grow callous and eventually insensitive to your points. (If they don't just buck and throw you off first!)

No whips allowed

Another animal-handling policy we had was "no whips." "Whips don't work" was Dad's stand on the matter. The closest thing we ever came to using one while herding stock was to rip off a willow switch or small tree branch and use it not to strike the animals, but to "whoosh" and "swish" through the air to keep their attention directed to the herdsman. Fortunately the same no-whip policy applied to us kids, although it did allow a little direct application of the willow switch when we deserved it for deliberate disobedience. We could generally move fast enough and jump high enough and yell loud enough that the swoosh was about all we felt, too.

It didn't take long in the barnyard to learn that whipping, beating, or kicking livestock never got you anywhere. An uncontrolled temper is not a nice or necessary quality in the barnyard or the boardroom. It should never be allowed or tolerated. I've seen angry, frustrated farmers beat defenseless animals using two-by-fours, chains, and pitchforks. I've watched the same thing in business as managers and owners use schedules and leverage to beat people to the floor, not realizing

that broken hearts don't bleed visibly. There is no reason or excuse for this on the farm or in the finest office.

Walk surely and you won't need a big stick.

Don't lie to your stock

Amazing how many people think they can get away with lying. A lie does the most damage to the one telling it, though the effects of this are often hard to see or understand unless you've worked with animals. Even the dumbest animal can see through a liar. I call it pan rattling.

One of my earliest responsibilities was to catch the horses in preparation for the day of toil. The horses, who roamed freely in a forty-acre pasture, were by no means ranked in the top ten of animal intelligence. But they did know that once they were caught in the morning, they faced a day of hard work. This made them difficult to catch, especially for a nine-year-old boy. Trying to run them down on foot in that large meadow was futile. So I poured a couple of tin cans full of oats or barley into a small pan and let the horses catch a whiff of it. When they came up to munch the fresh grain, I grabbed their halters and they were mine.

When catching time came around and I was short on oats, I'd resort to a clever trick. I'd carry the empty oat pan out to the horse area, then rattle it. The horses, seeing the pan and hearing the familiar sound, would come over to get their oats. As soon as they stuck their heads in the pan, I'd grab the halter.

This trick would work for three or four times without any grain, but soon the horses became smart enough not to fall for a no-reward situation. They refused to come, so I'd go and get some grain, lure them to me again, and reinforce my conditioning. When out of grain, I'd go back to empty pan rattling. This deceitful practice soon violated any semblance of trust the horses had for me. They finally wouldn't come at all, making them almost impossible to catch and causing me considerable loss of time and prestige with the drivers.

Likewise, we kids used to fill the manger full of hay, or our arms full of fresh alfalfa to trick cows into coming close enough for us to catch them. As soon as we had them, we tossed or took away the bait. To lure the little lambs and calves we used a bucket of diluted milk. It always worked a few times and then the critters would wise up and ignore us—they mistrusted us. It's pretty embarrassing to have a dumb sheep reject you, but anyone who lies deserves it.

Unkept promises of promotions, raises, transfers, and other perks are lies, too, and you know if you can't fool a pig or a cow, you sure aren't going to suck in an educated human. "Keeping your word" means *all* your promises, so don't just glorify the one in ten you did fulfill.

Too much green stuff ruins anyone

The modern corporation-climbing youngsters out in the business field act exactly like a bunch of yearlings out in a new pasture. They romp, kick up their heels, butt each other around, race and crowd each other, and of course, eat up all the opportunities at their feet. Much of this "growth" activity is harmless, except for the ever-present risk of bloat, which comes from too much green hay (or green money) too fast.

In the barnyard, at certain times of the year when the moisture level is just right and the alfalfa or clover is lush and green, it's all too greedily consumed by the enthusiastic cows. Then it ferments rapidly, and a lump the size of a basketball appears on the upper left side of their chest just behind the rib cage. This swelling, which is composed mostly of gases of fermentation, does more than make a cow uncomfortable—it presses against the lungs and restricts breathing. The cow is probably feeling pretty regretful right now for all that uncontrolled gluttony, as she stands there gasping for air. If her body can't manage to process all that greenery and the resulting gas, the cow's eyes roll and down she goes, to draw her last breath.

Many a farmer has had the agony, some dewy morning, of finding most of his precious herd lying on the ground like inflated balloons, with four stiff legs pointing upward. For that matter, even one bloated animal is a heartbreaking sight. Whenever we turned our herd into any potentially risky greenery, or even fed them dry but rich hay, one of us would stay around among the stock armed with a razor-sharp pocketknife. If any bloating appeared we wouldn't leave until the animal managed to belch (which would help relieve the pressure) or all "basketball sides" were flat. When a cow just couldn't handle it and fell to its knees dying, we'd move up to it and drive the point of the knife into the bulge. Air, partly digested feed, and manure would spray out of that small wound like a geyser, hitting you in the face. There was so much pressure it would whistle. The cow, having recovered a little lung room, would then gasp, breathe deeply, jump to its feet, run off a few yards, and look back at you with a blinking, sheepish expression.

I've often thought this crude but effective process would be the perfect cure for "business bloat"—all the pompous executives around who get so much green money so fast their system can't process it. They just seem to run or stand around bloated all the time, eating more and more. Overfed executives are probably the single greatest killer of businesses. We can't prick them with a needle, or take their money away from them without stampeding them. But we can stick them with *more to do* to help them work off some of that gas.

Rock picking

Idaho is rich in rocks, and every spring as the fields were prepared for planting, it seemed that more would appear. Rocks on or in a field could end up in the combine or other machinery and cause a breakdown.

To get rid of rocks, a horse or tractor would be hitched to a flat-top wagon and four to eight of us, depending on who was available or visiting, would follow the wagon through the fields, picking up any rocks we saw and tossing them on the wagon. There was lots of bending, lifting, carrying, throwing, and occasional arguments over whose rock was whose. This was great exercise out in the fresh air and wasn't mentally straining, so we would visit, daydream and race each other as we worked. When the tires on the wagon began to squash down, we'd jump on the wagon and ride to the rock pile and in competitive fury, unload it. Then back for another load, and another and another!

My ranch at McCammon, Idaho, has been picked many times, often with family or Scouts. Every project or bit of landscaping I've ever done here has meant rocks to pick, rake, break, or bury.

There are some good hints here for avoiding rocky seasons in business. No matter how well oiled or smooth an operation or administrative process is, little negatives like pettiness, paranoia, personal unrest, little office cliques and rebellions, unsafe practices, unnecessary expenses, and poorly thought out ideas or policies can crop up, and have to be picked—removed. If you ignore them, like the rocks, they get in the machinery and damage your business. A few bad accounting practices may have been ignored by one of the nation's largest accounting firms at first. Left continually unpicked, these rocks piled up and helped topple mighty Enron, ruining many innocent investors' lives in the process.

Rock picking is a necessity for survival, and if done well and regularly it cleans up the working field in business, as on the farm.

"Hired hands" don't solve everything

Most farms operate like most businesses begin, with just the family. Non-ag businesses grow faster and often need employees, lots of them, while a farm usually expands slowly enough for family to handle.

We ran an efficient farm and barnyard, and every minute and muscle was usually well accounted for. But sometimes when seasons were delayed or came early, someone was sick, or relatives and neighbors couldn't find time to help, the announcement would be made that we were going to get a hired man to help. The idea always seemed like salvation, but it was more like calling in a relief pitcher. You never really knew if the guy was going to win or lose for you. I remember once in the busiest part of spring Dad injured his back badly, to the point that he could scarcely crawl from the house to the barn. So a hired man was secured. Dad then had to spend two full days crawling

around showing the man what to do and where. The guy broke everything he touched, and the only bell that rang in his brain was the dinner bell. After the farm was set back at least two weeks, Dad decided the help was a bigger pain than his back and crawled through the rest of that spring working alone.

The majority of businesspeople today wouldn't consider crawling or enduring pain, and they do believe in hiring someone to "do the work" while they sit at a desk or drive around and rake in the profits. More people doesn't automatically mean more work done—it may mean that, but be prepared for some problems and disappointments. You'd be surprised how often getting the folks responsible right into the fields is the real solution.

Hardware disease

I remember a sick cow we had once, which after a visit to the vet lived to a ripe old age. The cow's ailment, we were told, was "hardware disease." Before that day I'd never heard of such a condition, but I was impressed and never forgot the vet's display of what he removed from the cow: little pieces of barbed wire, a bent nail, a bottle lid, etc. How do things like this get in a cow? They just gobble up whatever happens to be in the grass, the vet told us, and of course stuff like this can't be digested. Enough garbage in a cow long enough will kill it, he said; and this was a common occurrence on old farms.

How like that Holstein we are, as we gobble up whatever comes along in the interaction called business. We'll carelessly consume the barbs and bolts to get some green stuff, and then we have to pack all this around, because it's indigestible. Most contracts that you read, for example, give you the green, all right, but mixed in artfully with barbs like "first refusals" and "hold harmless" clauses. To get the green we eat the hardware—bad business. Pure green is possible; you don't always have to take the bad with the good. Check with someone knowledgeable and make sure there truly is no escape from the tough stuff before you ingest it. In business no one is going to come along and cut it out of us—it'll just do us in.

The difference between pushy and pleasant

Getting along with and getting respect from your peers is a basic survival skill of business, yet a lot of people seem to have two left hooves when it comes to this. Again, a little observation of the cow kingdom in operation will provide some guidance for those of us who occasionally have trouble being accepted.

First there is what we might call the "dumb" cow, and when it first arrives at the barnyard, all the cows (like all the office staff) look up. And some run over and stick their heads over the fence and bellow at it. The dumb cow is unloaded and pushed through the gate and immediately does a dumb thing. She puts her tail in the air, gallops into the middle of the herd, and in an attempt to assume instant status, butts and pushes the others aggressively to show that she has arrived and is important. The other cows tolerate, but hate, the dumb cow's actions and later at the feed manger, all will conspire to squeeze the dumb cow out, crowd her into the ravine, stand and block her way to water, and in all kinds of subtle ways make life as miserable as possible for her for as long as they can.

In contrast now let's look at the "smart" cow the farmer brings the next week. She gets the same initial mooing and sideways looks from all the resident stock. Once unloaded, through the gate, however, the smart cow just quietly and politely stands there and lets the other cows walk around her, sniff her, and look her over. Then she grazes apart from the herd, nipping the rejected grass along the fence or among the weeds, working around the edges, never crowding, pushing, or bullying. She just takes whatever's left over and gradually moves closer and closer to the main herd until one day she is one of them, maybe even a leader.

As kids we delighted in watching the smart and dumb cows operate, little realizing that they were teaching us an important lesson in business interaction. Namely, that acceptance has to be earned, it can't be forced. Relationships have to be given a chance to develop naturally. And the last thing you ever want to do is make the resident stock feel threatened or inferior. Too many new employees think their spots, horns, pedigree (degrees) or previous pasture (position) give them the "in" or the right to have it all instantly. As we can see, they're just asking for some butting around. Being a smart, humble cow is what really cuts it, in the barnyard or business.

Feed them right or they'll eat you up

Late one winter, Dad and I drove by a field where a farmer had seven horses fenced in a corner lot, and I guess he must have forgotten they were there, the way their ribs and hip bones showed though their skin. In desperation they were actually eating the fenceposts!

When you walk through a barnyard, likewise, you'll sometimes see poles or even parts of buildings that appear to be eaten away. You're seeing right—that's exactly what's happened. If stock has a poor diet or not quite enough food, to get minerals or just plain nourishment they'll often gnaw and nibble at all kinds of things, including valuable, expensive structures. Employees will do the exact same thing to you if you "starve" them with low pay, and lack of the critical mineral called "consideration."

A poorly looked after partner or employee (even family) working with or for you will start in on your posts and pillars, and in a not so subtle way, either. They'll think of it as a right, a well-deserved little dietary supplement, things like taking false sick days, permanently borrowing (stealing) stuff, cutting their hours a little here and there, abusing your equipment and vehicles, feeding negativity to their fellow workers, moving more slowly and limiting their performance to the lowest gear they can get away with, etc. A good nourishing balanced diet is as important for employees as it is for animals. If you notice some deterioration of your facilities and your workforce, check their diet (pay and benefits)!

You can't hide trouble

I bought forty acres of sagebrush near our ranch once, and developing it into five-acre ranchettes required that I build a road. My father, a former road construction foreman, came up to show my sons and me how to build a road, everything from dynamiting when necessary to dirt fill. I was about to bury a good-size mesquite stump with my scraper when Dad stopped the rig and fished it out. "You never bury anything rottable in fill," he said, "because someday it will be gone and the area will cave in." He said that when the Teton Dam on the Snake River had been built almost fifty years ago, they dozed timber in the fill, "and someday they will pay for it." This was ten o'clock on Saturday morning, and at noon we stopped to eat in Dad and Mom's motor home. The news was on, and there was an emergency for all of the people in the Snake River watershed—the Teton Dam had just collapsed, flooding a cattle feedlot and lumberyard and all of the towns below it. Talk about coincidence!

On a farm, as in a business, any unresolved issues will eventually have to be answered for, and by then they may be much bigger questions. A few little things out of place, temporary setbacks or disagreements or surface issues will often take care of themselves or work themselves out in time. But big, unresolved events, problems, or injustices, no matter how well hidden or buried, will cause an often invisible weakness, that could someday bring your whole business down.

Waiting time

The farm subtly introduced me to multi-tasking, the simple but efficient practice of cutting wasted time by using waiting time. Once water was "set" to irrigate a field on the ranch we had to wait for it to reach the end of the rows before leaving (to make sure it didn't spill over, all go down a gopher hole, etc.). Sitting around idle any time was unacceptable, so while in that vicinity we would repair fences, clean weeds out of nearby ditches, pick rocks and pile them up, sharpen shovels, hunt, etc.

Later, when my cleaning company crews were waiting for wax or paint to dry at the small telephone offices and installations we serviced, we would sweep sidewalks, kill weeds, clean equipment, clean vents, clean any nearby phone booths, remove snow from the roof or bird nests from the gutters, etc.—little jobs that often made extra trips necessary. This multi-task approach allowed us to provide ten or twelve services per trip instead of just one, and eventually establish a regular route and schedule of maintenance for these remote little offices, reducing the price of maintaining them and expanding profits for both us and our customers. (And leaving our competitors scratching their heads wondering why we got all the "rural" phone contracts.)

The blue-ribbon best of all business, management, and even life lessons

Between high school and college, I had more than 111 different teachers—instructors, coaches, tutors, and professors. Eight of them were inspiring and touched my life, another fifteen left some impression, and the rest were "chloroform on the hoof." When I think of

where most of the truly soul-stinging stuff came from, especially for good personal management, I'd have to put the plain old pig ahead of all 111 of them.

There's one big truth, for example, that you either learn and put into practice in business or you suffer and struggle. I learned it one afternoon from a pig. Since you all haven't had the privilege of raising hogs, let me point out first that they have four outstanding characteristics:

1. They get out. You can have the best fence money can buy or Barney can build, and if a pig can get its snout through it (even if it's made of battleship steel), that critter can and will get out.

2. Once out, pigs switch on their rooting radar, and they can and will find every flower or frill of value. What they don't eat they wallow in or tromp to death.

3. Pigs have no neck. They're built like a torpedo. That means there's no place to grab and catch one, once they're launched.

4. When chased, they travel like a torpedo. The only difference is that a torpedo takes a little time to gain full speed; a pig is there from step one.

By the end of my high school days I had seventy pigs, offspring from my FFA (Future Farmers of America) project. We had a big farm and old fences, so a loose pig or two occasionally was no surprise. But when they found Mother's mums or marigolds in the garden, those were dark hours. Following threats of fresh pork chops, we would go "get the pigs in." Much easier said than done. The showdown always

came at a corner in the fence, where ultimately any animal runs and sticks their rump against the corner post and looks you in the eye, awaiting your next move.

At this point we'd extend both arms to try and double our size and intimidate the animal. We'd close in on the cornered critter and then they'd make their move. You could only marvel at the speed—zipppp!—with which the "Oinkion Express" bolted right past you or between your legs, and any lunge or grab yielded only dust-covered straw or manure.

Many, many times those pigs outsneaked, outran, outmaneuvered, and outmanaged me, until one day, the great secret, the only thing any businessperson absolutely must know, was revealed to me. A pig was out again, and Mother was loading the shotgun and sharpening the butcher knife. I cornered the pig as usual, and as we looked each other in the eye, I closed in. The pig started to move toward the right, so I jumped to the right. He immediately shifted and prepared to go left, so I leaped left. Now the pig decided that maybe right was best after all, and he shifted his front legs to the right. Then I said to myself, "Man, I'm smarter than that pig, and I know what to do now."

So I crouched over with my arms out and headed toward that pig, shifting quickly and steadily side to side. The pig, getting confused and defensive now, started doing the same thing I was, shifting from side to side. As he shifted desperately from hoof to hoof and back again, trying to decide which way to go, I moved closer, and now we were nose to nose. I knew I had him, and it was time to close in for the catch. I was playing basketball in those days, and as a 5' 11" center I often had to fake those 6' 5" dudes out of their jocks, and now the big layup fake was the perfect thing. So I made a big fake to the left, and grabbed to the right, and aha! I had him.

I got so good at this that I let the pigs out on purpose, just to fake them out, take advantage of that prime weakness, *the inability to make a decision (until it's too late and then—bam!—bacon!).*

East Forty

Too much time waving

Most farm folks are known to be friendly and neighborly and "down home," and nothing is nicer than some well-chosen warm words in a visit. But nothing can make you poor faster, either, than spending too much time talking and waving. This is a real pitfall in both the barnyard and business.

One afternoon, Dad, my brothers and I were putting a corral up right next to a busy road. About the time we'd get a post or pole lifted up, someone would drive by and wave, and to wave back we'd have to drop the post or pole and then pick it up again. This happened again and again and then about every other post someone would slow up and stop and visit. Dad was friendly but he never stopped working, and he told us later, "You can be tuckered out by the end of the day just waving and visiting."

Now that I'm in business and have to do things like calculate production and labor costs, it's clear that his appraisal was pure wisdom. If you're going to get anything done you can't allow interruptions, polite or impolite. The barnyard was the perfect place to learn this because farmers all work at home, so people figure they can come, stop, and visit any hour of the day, and you'll just sit back and accommodate them. The fact that you're home must mean that you're off work, free. Would they ever think of stopping into a class at school and walking right up to the teacher and starting in: "How are things, Mrs. Penwick? How is the grading curve this year?" Never! Would they walk out to the pitcher's mound during the World Series and stop the windup to report on their wife's sister's new baby? Never! Would they walk into the operating room and stop the doctor and ask, "Well Harry, how many hernias have you handled this year?" Would they flag down Jeff Gordon in his racecar and ask him what kind of gas mileage he gets? Inconceivable, yet people will walk out into a field any day and stop a farmer on a $200,000 tractor to visit, or come into the barn during calving time and expect you to stop birthing to chew the fat.

When you stop in the barnyard or anywhere for idle chatter (and there'll always be all sorts of chances) the milk gets sour, the hay dries out, the customers move on to the next shop, etc.

Being friendly without being frozen (letting them stop your production) is the answer.

Keep your harness out of the rain

Have you noticed that poor managers, failing businesses, losing teams, discouraged people, and poor students all seem to have one thing in common? The way they care for their possessions, particularly their tools. Humankind's whole claim to fame has been defined as the ability to use tools, but if our tools are in bad shape, they don't work.

Losing your pocketknife, canteen, hoe, or shovel was bad enough in the barnyard, but if you ruined or damaged or put one of the crew's

tools out of commission, you were in big trouble! Besides two tractors, we worked with horses until 1953. So I learned to harness and unharness them when I was in fifth grade. And only once did I leave the harness outside on the corral pole. It rained, and Dad poured his wrath on me. He asked me if I'd ever tried to wear a leather glove that had been left in the rain and sun for a month. "Yes." "How was it?" "Painful." "Well wet, baked harnesses feel like that to a horse. And without a harness, a horse is just a hay burner."

"It's simple. You neglect and ruin the harnesses, and we can't work the horses. When horses don't work, crops don't get in. No crops, no money. No money, no food, shelter, basketball, dates, skates, or Roy Rogers shows—savvy?"

Now that he explained it all, I, even as a tender youth in the barnyard, could clearly see the connection between care of your equipment and life's purpose and pleasures. You keep your computer and camera clean and covered when you aren't using them, put the pliers back in the toolbox when you're done with them, and change the oil in motors, not because "it's a rule" or because you get paid to do it, but because it has a direct effect on your personal well-being. When something is ruined, lost, or fails to function because of neglect, even if no one knows about it or everyone else does it or the government or the boss owns it—*you* are the one who suffers in the end.

If your soil is shallow, supplement it!

Ask a farmer what his favorite field is, and the answer is just about sure to be: "bottom land." The rich, deep, level, well-watered land along watercourses can outproduce any other about three to one.

We all want a "bottom land" life. The best. To be able to do a lot, achieve a lot, feel a lot, and ultimately earn a lot of friends and funds. But often we discover our soil is shallow. We don't seem to have bottom-land brain or brawn. We aren't producing much; our life is just plain low yield. This common life and business occurrence is also common back on the farm. Some fields, as a result of constant use, abuse, and erosion, their mineral content or location, offer only a poor or limited yield.

With land (as with our own lives), we have some choices to make when the results of something aren't sufficient to justify the investment:

    1. Give up on it, move away from it or abandon it

BARNYARD TO BOARDROOM

2. Put it into permanent pasture
3. Keep on accepting the meagerness
4. Complain and moan louder, more often
5. Build it up to bottom land

Choices 1–4 are more common and easier, but number 5 is by far generally the best choice for the ground as well as the heart, the mind, and the muscle. Remember, the potential of wonderful growth and living is right there already, all in place, it's just a little short of some supplement. Back on the ranch we had fields that looked and laid beautifully but handed us skimpy crops, just as some of our fellow humans (maybe even ourselves) look and sound good but hand us skimpy results.

For the ground we first analyzed it, to find out what it had too much or not enough of, what it needed to build it up and balance it. Often, like us, it had lots of talent or potential (even too much) in one area but lacked in another. So we added fertilizer here and minerals there to complement what was there or compensate for what had either been lost or never been there. We rotated crops, added humus, sometimes we even gave it a rest (laid it off—no crops for a while). We tended it and nurtured it, and *always*, with the right care, it responded. In short, we subscribed to the philosophy of improving what we had instead of quitting, trashing it, or moving on. Go to any barnyard board meeting and have it explained. Tour a properly fertilized field, and look at the results come fall in the grain elevator or the corncrib. Do something, but don't live with shallow soil. You'll never have any kind of crop or life without servicing your shallow spots.

If you don't switch pastures, you'll ruin the grass

Many of us, at least once, have driven past a herd of cows or sheep on the road. In case you wondered, they're being moved from one pasture to another. Once the grass in a field is eaten down low, the stock, if not taken off it, will consume it right down to the roots and kill it. If you leave animals in one field too long, they'll also eat up all the more appetizing kinds of plants and leave only the tough, ugly, less nutritious stuff to reseed and take over.

A new pasture not only gives the cows a new outlook and taste, it lets the old grass grow back. I run my business that way. No matter how good or important a project is, if we don't switch off it for a while to a fresh place, project, or product, we seem to lose our momentum and enthusiasm. ("Rotation" is the Wall Street word for this.) If you wait too long and "eat a project down," like a pasture, it gets worn out and grows weeds too big and tough to handle. Cows love a change of stomping ground, and so will you and your people!

The barnyard champion team

Of all the teams we put together on the farm I always thought the best was the two Morgan workhorses we had. If the reins were in the hands of a good driver, their precision work was something to behold.

I wasn't married long before I realized the real truth of the matter. The best and most necessary team was a husband and wife! When they functioned in harmony their output was hard to beat. In the rural setting I grew up in, each had his or her own area to look after, but either could switch to and handle the other's operations if necessary. The dynamite president of one of the world's largest ag cooperatives once took a detailed tour of hundreds of dairy farms in the U.S. When asked what was the overall most consistent ingredient of the most successful ones, he said, "Without question, the dairies run by husband/wife teams were superior to all of the others. The two of them together seemed to have a joint scope of care that a platoon of hired hands couldn't muster. A committed and coordinated husband/wife team beat every professional manager or organizer I saw, not in just a few, but *all* cases." That was a significant observation!

As I approach my own fiftieth wedding anniversary, I wonder what "Dad's" farmyards and fields would have been like without Mother and can wholeheartedly endorse that co-op president's findings. What worked on the farm works in every other kind of business, too.

Slipknots choke!

I remember the day my uncle bought a magnificent new speckled workhorse, a big event in any barnyard. He tied him in the barn for the night, and the next morning, bad news—that perfectly healthy horse was dead. The knot around its neck was a slipknot and when the horse pulled, it tightened. As it became alarmed it pulled harder and the knot tightened more, until the horse strangled.

A horse seems at least four times its ordinary size when dead, and Grandpa, my uncles, Dad, and all us kids gathered around to see this astonishing sight. Shaking his head, someone said, "Just a simple knot." It should have been a bowline. Someone was careless and it cost.

People use slipknots in business constantly, words like: "might," "maybe," "I'll see," "I'll look into it," "later," "perhaps," "if," "we'll try," "we'll work on it," "pending," or "on hold." Business, too, slips and chokes when slipknots are used. A straight answer and an outright commitment is a firm knot—you might even call it a square knot.

Learn and use names

Dale Carnegie must have spent some time in a barnyard, because an important part of his advice for good diplomacy was to "learn and use names." Not only does every person have a name, believe it or not, every farm animal did too. They might be christened for their temperament (Bossy or Charger), coloration (Brownie or Ol' Red), or some distinctive feature (Limpy or Droop Ears), but using their name unquestionably helped to obtain obedience and gentle them down. It was the rule of our barnyard—and fun, too—that every animal had a name. I fed sixty Herefords or "whitefaces" and it didn't take too much imagination to see how each one of them resembled some person I knew, or even a star. I had Gary Cooper cows, Teddy Roosevelt cows, math teacher cows, and even Marilyn Monroe cows. Farmers who used only "Hey" or "you spotted SOB" struggled a lot more with their stock. Some horse teams thought their names were God and Damn.

Name recognition of your employees and coworkers will gain you not only attention and respect but time and efficiency. How often do we hear people refer to "that salesman" or "one of those clerks" as if it were "one of those horses" or "that cow?" We all have names and we all love to hear them, and even well chosen nicknames can perform a real function for both parties... *if* we use them.

Surrendering the keys

One winter morning, as we often did, we loaded some stock into the truck to take to market. Going to the stockyard with Dad was always a treat. But this time he tossed me the keys and said, "You take them to the sale—I'll be staying home," and walked away. My first solo trip!

The full weight of responsibility descended after I was alone with our "assets." The roads were full of black ice and several times I nearly lost control. I finally arrived and began the whole process of lining up, signing up, weighing, and bidding, and then picking up the money. I remember the mounting thrill as I got closer and closer to success, the relief of "done," and the confidence that came with it. The trust of this one little trip opened a lot of other life doors. Likewise, when Dad jumped off a machine, truck, or tractor and said, "It's yours—get it done," fear was always soon converted to confidence. I left the farm believing that there was nothing I couldn't do.

Turning loose the keys and saying, "It's yours—get it done," can be a real confidence booster for the people who help make your business operate, too. Confidence they gain in successfully completing smaller tasks will build to confidence for larger projects.

Of course, my black-ice trip to the stockyards wasn't my first trip there. From my previous trips with Dad I knew exactly what to do before, during and after the sale. Remember to make certain your employees know the road and the routine before they take off on their first solo ride.

> The process of developing good business results is a two-way chute—you give responsibility (trust in others) and you take responsibility (trust yourself).

Middlemen

The barnyard was a place of full responsibility and conservative profits. You never "made it" overnight and if you let something go you'd really know it. Many a time Dad would leave me with an important job so he could go somewhere and buy parts. The minute he left I'd go to my little brother and bribe and coax him with all kinds of goodies to do the job for me. Call it delegation, or attempted middleman status, if you will. It always seemed like a good idea to get someone else to do the job while you raked in all the benefits.

The problem was, it seldom worked. My brother would goof off or forget and Dad would arrive with the job still undone. I'd be called a worthless little snot and have to go do it myself anyway. Even if you've assigned or delegated something, *you're* still responsible for getting it done.

It took years for this to sink in, and I'm glad it finally did. Delegation, in truth, is often kind of the comforting illusion that something is being done until you have time to take care of it yourself.

Delegation is a great and effective concept when used wisely, but it sure isn't *the* answer to getting things done. It isn't assurance that something will be done the way or when you like, or even that it'll be done at all. And delegation isn't free; you pay for those you send on your errands.

Delegation is easy to preach from the business pulpit, but tricky to put in practice. So especially don't count on it as salvation for those "too late" or "too hard" situations. Delegation is often badly used in business when people get an overload. If someone in the company caused that overload, he or she ought to put in free overtime and take care of it, instead of "delegating it" at someone else's expense.

The same goes for paying for outside expertise—a good idea, if the person or firm in question truly is an expert and if the advice is really necessary. When Dad first bought cattle he used a cattle buyer, who supposedly always knew where the best cows were for the best price. He'd get them and then take a commission for his work and wisdom. He did an okay job, but got sloppy after awhile, began running late and sometimes delivering a bad count, so Dad ended up just buying direct.

It makes sense to pay for people to help you do a job, as long as they do help. But pay attention—just because they're certified or licensed doesn't mean they live up to that commission or finder's fee.

This kind of "delegation" isn't a sure cure for anything, either. I've listed land with real estate agents, for example, who never turned a hand. I ended up finding the buyers and selling the property and paying them thousands of dollars in commission. Business is overburdened with middlemen of all kinds: agents, consultants, buyers, brokers, wholesalers, etc. Before you know it there are scores of these between you and the product, and they aren't there for free. They need pay or commission for what they do, and you'll find as I did with my little brother, that it's easy to promise perks to someone before the job, but after it, when paying time comes, it's always hard to divvy up the dough, no matter how small an amount it may be.

The more mane, the more burrs

When businesses reach the straining point they always make cuts, a procedure well known in the barnyard. Long manes and tails gather lots of burrs, a nuisance no horse or farmer needed, so we kept our horses sheared and sharp, with tails long enough to swish flies, but short enough to prevent debris collection. Likewise, silver buckles and flashy decorations on saddles or harnesses look good at a rodeo or parade, but only threaten both production and safety on the job. Strip them off and your mount will love you for the weight loss.

Trimming excess is important in any business. As neat or attractive as unneeded niceties may be, when the competition heats up, they do have to be trimmed. Business "fat" often carries the pleasantly vague name of "overhead." A lot of it is vanity expenditure that doesn't wear well in the end and only becomes unnecessary burden. I meet so many people in business who struggle because they're so focused on and fascinated by "image" and accessories they never get to the purpose of what they're doing. Many learn too late that even a good business can't feed too many fineries. Finding beauty in the basics is a real key to running a successful business.

Decoration takes a lot of upkeep, too, which means time taken away from the productive heart of business. It took hours of combing and currying to deburr a horse back on the ranch, and they hated every minute of it. I've found the trim principle even worth applying at the personal level: By keeping my hairstyle short and simple, and not carrying any jewelry, cosmetic, or habit baggage, I can get ready in the morning almost half an hour faster than many of my business associates, who have to fumble around with a hair dryer, aftershave, rings, necklaces, and two cups of coffee just to get them going. Simplicity doesn't mean suffering, it means freedom to get on with what life's about!

"Predictability"—a skill you've got to have

Experience is a good teacher, *if* you learn from it. Some of us have twenty different experiences in a day; others have the same experience twenty times.

Being able to anticipate outcomes, so you can alter the direction of things to your benefit, is essential in running a business. In fact failure is almost inevitable without it. Thousands of businesspeople bumble along doing business, waiting to see how things will come out instead of making them come out the way they want. Whenever in the thoughtlessness of youth, my brothers or I would build a weak fence or irrigation dam, leave a bolt loose, fail to cover a feed bin, try to work with a broken tool, drive on a low tire, drink too much ice water on a hot day, or overheat the horses—Dad would ask only one question, "Now just what do you think is going to happen?" Taking this a step further, if before any undertaking you stop to think, "What am I going to do if _____?" and prepare for it, then change things around a little if you need to, you'll save half a day's work, and sometimes a lot more. In business we now call this contingency planning; back then we just called it predictability, knowing what would or might come about and being ready for it.

When I drove animals to move or load them, they'd seldom go exactly where I was trying to get them like they always did for Dad. It was all the skill of predictability. Dad would stay back a little farther from the critter than I did and instead of drowsing along (like too many business leaders do), he watched the eyes, head, tail, and hooves of the animal. And he would know, by the movement of a muscle or other subtle little signs, precisely when they were thinking about bolting or turning wrong. And just ahead of their move Dad would make his, a quick step to the right or left and the critter would change course. It was marvelous.

I now spend most of my planning time predicting and preparing for moves, and haven't had to do a major roundup for years!

Stay clear of tight situations

How many people drown trying to save someone from drowning? Most of the time, jumping right in with someone in trouble is real dumb; you always want to use a rope, pole, or other tool. Then let them grab onto that, and you might save them.

To survive on the ranch, likewise, you learned to care for and control things while still keeping a safe distance between you. Many a farmer has been caught and almost crushed to death by heavy equipment, a load of grain, or an animal—because they got too close. When you do that your options and choices are limited, if not eliminated.

Companies and individuals you work with in business can end up in some real "tight spots" (business and personal trouble). If they want to involve you, it may be part of your responsibility, or you may just want to try and help. But keeping your hand on the rope and keeping a good distance between you and the problem is generally the smartest, safest way to solve it. You won't get pulled in, and then have to dig yourself out or untangle yourself. If someone at work has a financial, romantic, or attitude problem, if you jump right in with him or her you risk compassion turning to passion and then suddenly you'll be part of the problem, not part of the solution. The old "Don't bring the hungry food, teach them how to fish for their own" principle is a much better idea here. When you're in too deep you can't control the outcome.

The barnyard principle of keeping yourself in the clear will serve you well if you follow it. Help, but don't get so close that you're helpless, too.

"It's not my job..."

One of the reasons the work went so well, and you whistled and sang while you worked there, was that barnyards when I was growing up were never unionized. There were no limits on what, when, how, or how much you did, or for that matter who did it. We all had our own job assignments, but if any job wasn't done, and you happened to be on the scene, it was *your* job. You'd only have to say "But that ain't my job" once to earn severe consequences (not only for using "ain't," but for complaining about a little extra responsibility). It may seem unfair at the time to "pick up the slack for a slacker," but think about it a minute. Maybe the designated worker was sick, had an accident, car trouble, or a family problem—or was simply overloaded or stuck on another job on the South Forty. Doing something for someone else can be a genuine pleasure, as long as you aren't being asked to do it daily.

On the farm we'd never leave someone behind to finish up "their" job while we went in to bed or to dinner. We all jumped in to help finish the last row of beets or the shucking, and even if all of "our" regular cows were milked we'd take on some extras till they all were done.

The sooner you and your employees adopt the following attitude, the sooner good things will start happening for everyone: "I'm happy to do anything I can do to help my colleagues, because it only helps all of us and the company."

Who can hurt you most

In the barnyard we had critters that could inflict some heavy damage on you: huge horses, bulls, tusked boars, rams, and roosters. These might look the most ferocious, but it was the gentle females with little ones at their side who could really clean your clock. "Mad mothers" were deadly. Once there was a baby involved you'd better keep your distance. I barely escaped many a snorting charge while attempting to move a mother and her offspring. You get on the bad side of a female with someone to protect and you have a battle no bull

can match—they'll fight to the death, preferably yours. They'll charge, kick, and tromp on you, and when you get your distance, they'll run back to their space and stare you down. A mad mother whose territory you invade in any way will really put the hurt on you.

At work, plenty of people are just grazing or chewing their cud or taking in the scene. But there are some, like the mother cow or a dog with a new bone, who have something to push or protect. They've staked out a territory or a title, committed themselves to a course or a cause. These are the ones to tread wisely around. (And stay ready to perform the wisest action of all—which is usually RUN!)

Bad smells don't always mean bad outcomes

Odor can blank out our business brains, and "reek havoc" with potential profits! All activities have an aroma, and especially when things are working away hot and heavy, it may not be good. We hear things like, "Get a whiff of that!"

We write off or avoid some great deals because of smell. My nose for business was developed in the barnyard where most of the stuff that smelled bad to outsiders (beet pulp, silage, manure, horse lather, and diesel fuel) was positive in the profit picture and often for the environment, too. Delicate and aristocratic folks who turn up their noses at a whiff of something unpleasant or unfamiliar won't ever know that some stenches are almost sacred. Stink is relative to function, and mother nature doesn't perfume her processes. The processing of gold ore really stinks, too, but when you get the gold, the process smells pretty doggone good!

Watch who you follow...

One of the most surprising lessons I learned on the farm was that even smart animals will follow a stupid lead animal. One morning, for example, I drove a herd of cattle up to a gate to prepare for a pasture transfer. We weren't in a rush, and having done all this many times before, they were just standing there contentedly, looking forward to the fresh new grass. Every herd, however, has a few hyper types or troublemakers. One of these suddenly bolted from the herd and leaped like a rabbit right into the middle of a canal. There was a huge splash, and then a lot of struggling and wallowing to get out, and then the cow ran down and stuck itself belly deep in the mud of the drainage swamp. There was no grass or really even anything to drink there; it was just a mucky slough.

What did the rest of the normally intelligent cows do then? They arched their tails and leaped into the middle of the canal, wallowed out, mucked through the swamp, and caught up with the lead cow. Then they all turned and looked back at me with a dumb look on their faces like: "Why did we do that?"

I watched episodes like this again and again in the barnyard and it proved to be a pattern I saw repeated when I moved into the business world. All will be calm and content in a company or corporation and suddenly someone will clamp onto a cause and start talking and complaining about it, and a whole herd of others will do the same. Or someone will bring free booze, or a proposal for a new betting pool into the office and everyone stampedes to participate. Later they'll turn around like the cows and say, "Gadfrey, why did we do that?"

The herd mentality poses as many problems in business as it does in the barnyard. The lead cow is not necessarily the best or the brightest, only the first and bravest (which can also mean most foolish). But sad to say, she is usually followed faithfully.

So set yourself apart from the herd, and carefully check out any lead cow before you decide to imitate her. If you don't run with the herd, you won't eat dust or get trampled. And while others are milling around admiring the latest fashions, sharing the latest viruses and the latest dirty jokes, squeezing in to get their share of a not very appetizing cake or big tray of fattening pastries, we can trot away from the crowd and do what we really want to do, what's right and proper— and profitable!

Empty corrals still cost

There are times in any barnyard when some of the stock or even all of it is sold, and the place is quiet and empty. Dad always planned for this and had new critters in there pronto. If he didn't he'd pace and fret around, much to Mom's irritation. When Mom would tell him to calm down, he'd always say:

"Empty corrals still cost money."

Then he'd explain that all the feeders, fences, haying machines, tractors, tools, and trailers, and all of our inventory of feed, had to be paid for and maintained whether we had any cows or not. Interest, taxes, depreciation, and rents continue, too, whether you have stock or not. If a corral was empty for six months, you paid out X dollars without any dollars coming in. Slowly it became clear that earning a pile of money, and then laying low for a while to use it up, just isn't good business. A corral is overhead, and for some reason it takes us all years to learn this lesson about overhead.

In my own cleaning company, for example, many of my managers have told me during the first two weeks of the month telling me that their profits are up beyond all expectations. "Don, we had two great commercial carpet cleaning jobs, made $1500 profit on one and $1000 on the other, so we have over $2500 profit this month." That day maybe he had, but then figuring he had things made, the fellow would waste the second two weeks and end up devastated, with a $1500 net loss for the month. Now I'd find myself explaining the corral principle of fixed costs—his own and his office helper's wages, his office rent, and his truck payment added up to $220 per day, which meant that if he made no further income, the very first day after the $2500 bonanza that he didn't work, he'd only made $2,280 for the month, by the end of the next inactive day only $2060, the next, $1840, etc. The overhead (empty corral) would eat up his profits.

An empty apartment, motel room, or office building likewise doesn't just sit there for free. You pay for the heat, lights, water, taxes, and mortgage whether the space is rented or used or not. Once you understand the empty corral concept, you understand where much of the pressure and stress originates for businesspeople. Learning it early, down on the farm, sure made it easier to see things clearly in the boardroom.

> The very first window cleaning job I ever did as a pro cleaner was five miles away from home. I had no car or equipment, so I bought a cake of Bon Ami and a bucket, borrowed a ladder and rag from my landlord, and walked to the job. When I got there the first thing I heard was:
> "What do you charge?" I was so nervous I could hardly answer.
> Finally: "$1.25 an hour."
> "Okay."
> It was October in Idaho, cold. I hustled and had the job done in two hours. The woman gave me a check for $2.50—all mine. Then I walked the five miles back to my dorm. Lots of people chuckle when I tell them this story, but today I have to do more than a hundred dollars worth of work to make the same $2.50. Business calls it inflation or overhead; back on the farm we called it "chaff."

Rake hay while the moon shines

Yes, you read it right—it wasn't "Make hay while the sun shines!" Not that the old saying isn't good, often well-taken advice. Once hay is

cut and down, you better get it processed and up in the stack quick. If it rains, the hay as well as the schedule will be ruined. A great lesson in expediency, but let me give you even a better one.

With both hay and business projects, once they're on their way you don't always have enough hours of sunshine. And if hay, for example, is down too long after it's cut, it'll dry out so much that when it's handled the leaves will fall off, leaving nothing but tough old stalks.

In a good business or any realm of accomplishment, there can't really be any "set hours" or off hours or after hours. Learning to work whenever the work needs done (not just during regular working hours) is one of the greatest secrets of farm and business success. Real accomplishment doesn't follow the clock or calendar; it follows **need**. When you need to, rake by moonlight. While the moon is shining is a great time to rake hay, because the dew keeps the leaves supple and attached.

In any kind of work, after a hard day, there are times when you want—and need—to put in a hard night, too… while the moon shines.

Get rid of rats

Many barns and lots of businesses harbor these little characters; sneaking, scurrying little dudes who thrive in unkempt environments.

"A clean barn leaves little for a rat to do, and nowhere for him to live," was our motto in the barnyard, and boy does it ever fit business. Let chaos, backlogs, and entanglements become part of your operation and rats, with their shifty little eyes, move in. Then you have employees who can't be trusted, who cheat, steal, tattle, sneak behind your back, and re-route everything into their own channels. ("You dirty rat," as Bogart used to say.)

If a rat chews his way into your chicken house, corncrib, or corporation, and you merely stop or block up the hole, you're only inviting a whole series of additional holes—probably in places that are harder to patch than the first one. You've got to catch the rat!

Rats do no more good in an office than they do in a barn, and any means is legal to dispose of them. Back on the farm, besides keeping the place picked up and clean, we had two other effective weapons for de-ratification—a .22 rifle and the barn cats. I put my rifle away when I went to business and retired my barn cats, too, but I didn't forget that the best way of all to keep rats away is simply to keep things neat and clean. This is one of the reasons for my deep-down love of cleanliness and order. Rats can't function or flourish in an open, honest environment, and that's the only way to run a business.

Don't spread it too thick!

The idea of fertilizer was a great mystery to me at age sixteen. Ground grew things anyway—how could a mist of spray or whisk of white powder out of a store-bought sack make any difference? The soil conservation man told us that not enough fertilizer would mean a weak yield, and too much would be so powerful it would "burn" crops. Money was scarce in those postwar days and Dad would buy giant loads of fertilizer, $1000 or more. My heart would sink every year he'd get conned into this.

How could I convince Dad, or satisfy myself on this? Well, the proving ground was at hand as I was sent to a fifteen-acre field with a pickup load of nitrogen phosphate and the drill set for 421 pounds per acre. When I finished I had a few sacks left over. Dad was 2000 acres away, so I loaded up the drill again, went to the middle of the field, and drove around in a perfect 200-foot circle, making several rounds in exactly the same place. I laid a layer of "Moregrow" on that ground that looked like a sheet of snow. A quick harrowing and the field was fertilized. I had my science experiment activated.

Dad planted Lemhi wheat, which comes up in ten or twelve days. A strange green ring appeared in the center of the field within a week, and then as the rest of the field grew the ring turned yellowish, as if the growth were stunted. Our house overlooked the field and Dad and the soil man were baffled. I said nothing, except to suggest that perhaps a flying saucer had set down some night. We had a nice four-foot high, eighty-five bushels to the acre yield in the rest of the field, all except my control area, which grew only six inches high.

The next year (Dad prepared the field this time) the wheat in the center grew green and thick but short. Two years later it grew six feet tall, like a tree, and didn't form a kernel. I was a believer!

The proper amount of fertilizer—elements that help grow your business—whether that means time and money to keep your machinery updated and functioning properly, or benefits that keep good em-

ployees loyal—will ultimately keep your venture productive. However, spreading it on too thick, as I learned here, can lead to no productivity at all!

Sell the steak, not the sizzle

Selling ahead of yourself, taking advances up front, on speculation, never has sat well with me. Grandpa always told me never to take a man's money till after you've delivered. Selling a product before it was ready, working out of the hole, so to speak, has always seemed a negative and possibly misleading proposition. "Don't call the cattle until you have the feed ready" was the code of the corral, for there's nothing worse than a herd of mooing stockholders all hyped to feast on "what is coming" or "what may happen." Putting the feed in the manger with 75 head already there reeling and grabbing is twice as tough as when it's clear.

I never really gave this much thought until I had my waterloo at the watering trough. It was my job to feed the skim milk from the cream separator to a hundred feeder pigs. The plan was to carry the milk to the trough in two 5-gallon containers, pour it in, yell "Pig, pig, pig," and then run out of there fast. Pigs are pretty enthusiastic about food, especially milk, so you could count on them coming quick. The secret of this particular job was not to call, or even let the pigs know you or the food were there, until it was served.

This particular evening I picked up the two pails of milk and headed for the barnyard. I got to the gate of the pen and set the buckets down to let myself through. The trough was still a good ways away out in the feed yard, and when I set the pails down softly the metal bale on one of them fell down and hit the side of the bucket with a little clink. All hundred pigs were burrowed and buried under the straw in the loafing shed about thirty yards away, and one single pig spotted me. It raised its head, looked around, and made a grunt that I imagine meant "soup's on."

I'd figured out months ago that if they beat me to the trough I'd never feed them. I had one choice: go for it. The minute I grabbed those two buckets back up the whole floor of the loafing shed rose up on 400 legs so close together there was still a blanket of straw over the top. That moving mass of meat headed for the table, and it was a tie. Those pigs weighed at least 170 pounds apiece and a hundred of them hit me and that milk full speed. The fresh scent of milk flew into the air, and they leaped all over each other and me in their frenzy. I was now thoroughly bruised and caked with pig manure, and I tried to beat them back with the empty buckets. This only spurred them on and further excited them, and from the black and blue of this experience I really absorbed the lesson: "Don't break the news till it is the news."

I see people sell books they haven't written, borrow on crops they haven't planted, and collect payments before they're earned. This is like asking to be paid for thoughts and dreams. In a few cases it may be the best way to go, but in general if we let some of the hot air out of business, we'd all breathe better.

When you overfeed, you waste

WHAT to feed the stock has been pretty well established by tradition, nutritionists, and the commonly available crops. "How much" is the critical concern of both rookie and veteran stockmen. The quality of the fodder involved, the weather, the age of the animals in question, and how often they're being fed all has a bearing, too, on how much you feed. I fortunately didn't have the responsibility of deciding. I just fed what Dad told me: eight bales in the morning, ten bales at night.

How did Dad know how much to give? By the waste! If the cattle licked the manger bare and the corral was broken down with the cows all over the stack, they needed more. If hay was left behind or pulled out of the manger, nibbled on a little, and then dropped and trampled

into the manure, we were overfeeding. Either extreme hurts both stockman and stock. Hitting and keeping the happy medium was important. There were some fine points here, too—for example, even though the number of cows usually stayed the same, on cold days they ate and needed more. Hay at $30 or $40 a ton then was expensive—it only took 25 eighty-pound bales to make a ton, so waste was out of the question.

It only took me a few years in business to discover that the same principle applied to the care and feeding of employees. Either extreme hurts the boss and the employee: Not enough, and they grow weak and discontented, and eventually break out and leave. Too much (free time, money, perks, privileges, advances, days off, tolerating of substandard work) and they'll take you for granted and waste your resources—act like they want more, but then just trample it underfoot.

Few can handle, or are grateful for, overfeeding. Mostly they'll just quickly adjust to that level of intake and output, and the more they get the less they'll thank you. Just enough—and an honest and accurate estimation of need—is best for both sides in the barnyard and business.

Don't stockpile trouble

I've been asked over and over what inspired me to write my bestsellers on junk and clutter, such as *For Packrats Only* and *Clutter's Last Stand*. Somehow, somewhere, I became intimately acquainted with the problems posed by excess "stuff," indoors or out. And yes, it was the barnyard. In *Clutter's Last Stand* I made it clear that farmers are the #1 junkers. (Junk, in case there's any doubt in your mind, is all those ugly, obsolete, useless things we have all over our homes and offices and yards, and packed into our attics, basements, garages, and closets.) As I said in *Clutter's Last Stand*:

Farmers have one distinct advantage over town junkers: They have more room to spread it out. They can distribute it eloquently from the North Forty to "out behind the barn." They have silos, barns, sheds, cellars, and granaries all available to store junk—and they do. Because room is no problem, farmers keep everything—including old tractors, machines, and vehicles. They just park them farther out in the field each time. They keep them for parts, of course, and the ancient 1880 junk they keep to snare a dumb city slicker who'll come along and pay $500 for a rusty milk can or warped wagon wheel.

Most farmers keep their old work boots so long that they can walk off by themselves, and the old gloves, hats, jackets, and coveralls they keep, alone, could stuff a silo. They have enough bolts buried somewhere to bolt together an aircraft carrier, and as for tools, most have a $70,000 inventory. Yet they keep the wire and string from every bale of hay, and every bucket, can, barrel, sack, and container that ever ambled onto the place. And once a farmer owns a blowtorch, nothing is junk. Everything—even an old license plate frame broken in four places—is kept because with a torch and welder you can make or repair anything and must have scrap metal around. I've seen farmers cut some good metal off an old truck bed and then keep the whole flaking skeleton for years, secure in the thought that they'd be able to pry a 10-cent lock washer off it someday... if they ever need it...

The big problem with stuff left in barns, sheds, yards, or fields is that it began depreciating the day it arrived. Iron and steel rust, and wood and fabric rot. Fragments and pieces get trampled and spread all over. But the barnyard somehow seems to be the ideal place to haul or drag some useless item so it can either restore itself or disappear. Neither happens, of course, and the heap keeps getting higher and kids and livestock are always being injured on it.

Dad's one descriptive word—"trashy"—said it all for things like this. And after I got out into the world of business I realized the barnyard had no corner on trash and clutter. Warehouses, shops, and offices, back rooms, lockers, and lofts, desks, tables, file cabinets, and supply cabinets all accumulate plenty. Enough obstacles and emergencies come up in the course of ordinary operations to keep things complicated—we don't need to stockpile trouble.

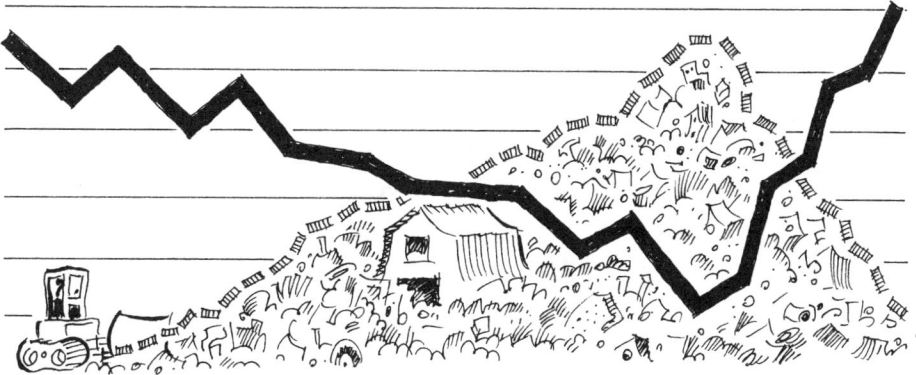

Every home or commercial building my company ever cleaned took a lot longer when stuff was piled all over: on the floors, on the furnishings, in all the corners of the rooms, and in the halls. As on the farm, all this not only makes the place look bad, it takes up space far better used for something else. It slows us and our employees down and makes us inefficient, makes us feel dumpy, provides a home for pests, and poses a safety hazard, too.

Dejunking doesn't cost anything—just a little time—and you'll find it one of the most profitable moves you ever make.

Buckers get sold

Some horses down at the old corral were like some employees, "buckers." Every time you tried to work with them, before they settled down and worked they just had to buck you. A little spirited snorting and prancing and a negative whinny or two is okay when a new policy comes along, but those who have to buck everything, every time, get real tiresome to have around. And they're seldom kept around— they're generally sold or even given away. A good lesson in cooperation.

(Some did learn to stick to the job later... as glue!)

Stubbornness just gets you clobbered

If we were ever caught beating an animal in the barnyard, we were in danger of getting the same with the same weapon. That sure isn't how things are done around most farms. There are some truly stubborn animals who will refuse to go in, out, or anywhere, even to be fed or helped, and like the proverbial mule, they just dig in and become immovable, unreasonable, and unyielding. First they get yelled at, then pushed and pulled, then slapped with a hand, and then with an old board, the weapons increasing with the farmer's temper and the amount of time wasted. I've seen animals beaten to their knees, looking back with glazed, frightened eyes, not knowing why this was being done to them and yet refusing to budge in spite of the pain.

I hate to see things hurt, so I always hoped you could somehow coach a problem cow or calf not to be stubborn, but it never seemed to penetrate that thick horned head. I learned from this, however, that stubbornness for any reason, right or wrong, is a real turnoff to anyone you have to work with. Refusing to budge or reason, even if you are right, will only get you "beatings" and even more unreasonable behavior back from others. Sticking to your guns is an admirable principle, but far better to clearly and calmly present your reasons for not wanting to do something, before it gets to the point of push and pull.

This kind of thinking:

I'm right; I have a right to be stubborn
I'm rich; I have a right to be stubborn
I'm smart; I have a right to be stubborn

isn't going to get you anywhere in business.

A person's word eliminates a lot of paper

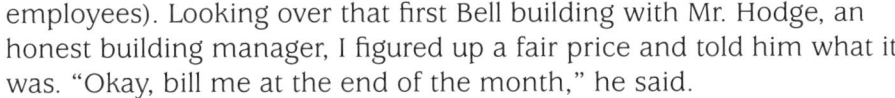

More than forty-five years ago I had the honor of cleaning the first Bell System building ever contracted out to a professional cleaner. Before this, all of their thirty-some thousand buildings were serviced in-house (by their own employees). Looking over that first Bell building with Mr. Hodge, an honest building manager, I figured up a fair price and told him what it was. "Okay, bill me at the end of the month," he said.

Without any formal agreement, contract, or written offer, we began cleaning that building for the biggest company in the world. Later, we made up a one-page outline of our duties and the price. Today, to contract the same job, to do the same cleaning of the same building, the contracts, clauses, riders, indemnities, insurance proofs and other protections, liability certificates, options, and compliances needed are thicker than a telephone book and involve more than forty people (lawyers, accountants, safety directors, security people, etc.) in addition to the principals, at now many times the expense.

The failure to use and honor the handshake costs our economy and ecology billions of dollars a day. Dumb, isn't it? Anywhere I can find a handshake deal I'll pay more up front and still save money. The best paperwork-reducing act going is to replace the pencil with an honest paw. Your "word" can and will save thousands of words on paper.

An honorable handshake saves a lot of time, and is one of the real secrets of success in business. Potential liability issues, and sometimes law or policy may require written agreements to protect your investors' investments. But there are still lots of deals, especially when you are paying cash as in the good old farm days, when a handshake is equally binding. (The trick is being sure you're dealing with people who honor handshakes.)

The curse of the corral, the exception

"Gee Mom, just this once..."

It worked sometimes, too! And once Mom made an exception to something (she didn't want to, she knew better), we made her pay. "One time won't hurt" might even be true if it did only refer to the single situation at hand, but as we all know violation of principle and practice soon becomes a habit and we move on to bigger and better exceptions. A little at a time is barely noticed, and it inflicts no pain, but the tally is always there and someday it's totaled. Like sneaked long distance phone calls or eating chocolates, each little exception is so small, so innocent, so enjoyable, until weigh-in time or the end of the month. If no accounting ever came, we could go on forever. But the end of the month and the end of the year always does come. Especially in business, there is a P & L, a balance sheet being made, whether it's on paper or not.

Neither businesses nor barnyards can tolerate many exceptions— they always add up in the bottom line at the sale yard.

Green hay can get hot!

One winter afternoon, Dad rushed into the house and hollered: "Grab some hay knives and come on, all of you." We followed him to the haystack on the run.

"Feel that," he said, pointing to a broken bale in the middle. I did and yeow, it was red hot. "It's spontaneous combustion," he said, "we have to rip this stack down and give it air to dry inside or it's going to burn down." Amazing that this innocent, beautiful alfalfa could ignite and burn months after it was cut and stacked. The reason was that it didn't have enough time to cure—it was baled green, with too much moisture in it. With time and compaction then came chemical reactions that generated enough heat to burn.

Likewise, when I first started to expand my business, I found that I made some mistakes with some of my managers. I stacked them somewhere before they were cured and seasoned, and with time and pressure they burned up on me.

Every farmer is overanxious, once the hay is cut and down, to get it up before bad weather. Nonetheless the wise and good ones wait, feel, and test until the hay is truly ready to be processed. Sending a green employee into an important business assignment is likewise a bad move. We may survive, as some of the smoldering stacks do, but it's costly.

Cash is more comfortable than credit

Mid life and waist deep in "business," I found myself spending at least three hours a day fighting finance—collecting (or trying to collect money due me), borrowing, arranging for payroll, advances, bonds, inventory, payments, etc. The fun of business left when worrying about cash flow became the dominant matter at hand. Like most other businesspeople I'd slowly slipped into a credit world, operating ahead of myself on would-be and long-range funds and profit. It was the progressive business "thing to do." I was 90% credit and 10% cash.

Back on the farm my folks (uncles and aunts, parents and grandparents) seldom talked or battled money worries in a big way, because they were the reverse, 90% cash/10% credit. They were way ahead of we modern financiers, because they lived off what they had, reality, instead of what might be, projections. They lived off last year's crops instead of next year's.

Today we live ahead of what we have, are, and can do, and it costs us plenty. They saved and then bought or built. We buy and build and then try to find creative financing to save us. What a stressful way to live! Cash gave them control of their time and money. They had less, but what they had they actually owned; they didn't have to submit to scrutinies, forms, statements, audits, and multiple signatures every time they wanted a dime or two. We slip into credit slowly, from con-

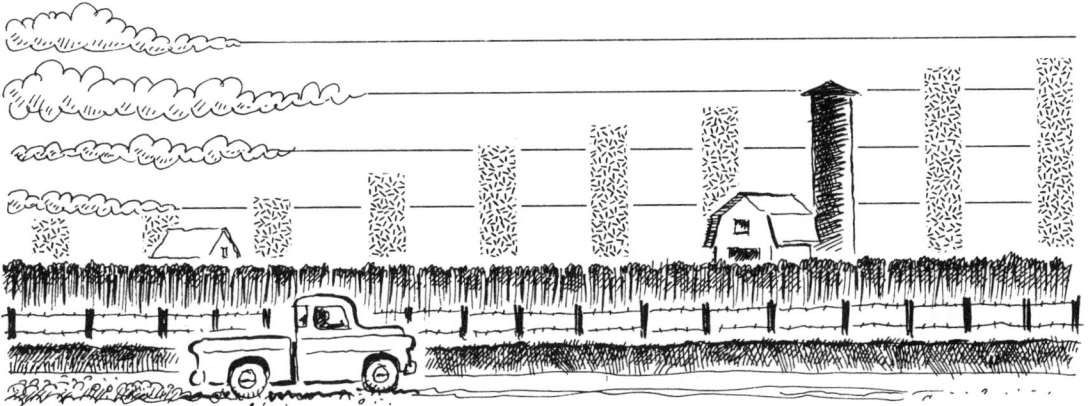

venience or necessity, and it ends up a thumbscrew if not a blocking of our main arteries. Cash was always so quick, clean, and committed. You didn't have to worry about papers and payments and scheduling and watching out for when the payment fell due. Credit is legal but it isn't very tender—it's kind of "procrastinated paying" and it has a lot more liabilities than the money it costs (the amazing amount—read the finance declaration—we end up paying by the time something is "paid off").

Buying a building or whole farm does take some time and usually some wise use of credit, but for those one-time or one-party deals, a few more cash transactions will brighten your attitude towards mornings, mail, and money, as well as many of those innocent days of the month.

You can't horse around with authority

Eight-year-olds love grandpas, and mine was generous, too, and promised me a horse. Grandpas tell the truth, so one day soon after he pulled in with our horse. I was little and trusting and had watched Roy Rogers and Hopalong Cassidy, so I couldn't wait! Soon the horse was out of the trailer and my cousin, Pat, and I were "legged" up onto it. We were straddling the horse and we kicked it in the flank as we were told to get it going. Soon it was galloping and believe me, sitting bareback on a moving horse isn't as easy as it looks in the movies—we soon leaned, slipped, and fell into a rolling heap.

This first equestrian experience didn't exactly launch a great relationship between me and horses. Before long I fell off several more times and got bit, as well as good and sore. By now Dad was saying horses had me "buffaloed," so I decided to enter and endure a horse trail ride. Right in the middle of some deep brush my horse and one of the others started kicking and biting at each other, and I didn't know what to do to stop it. Within seconds the horses were plunged into a ferocious fight. Both riders and both horses went down, one of the horses fell on us, and we all ended up caught and tangled in the brush. Hoofs were flashing around fast and striking some fancy blows and the other rider and I were scared out of our wits and happy to escape alive.

About this same time, I noticed that when our horse teams were being driven by Dad, they walked faster and pulled harder. As soon as I took the reins they knew it and started plugging and shuffling along. I lowered my voice in an attempt to sound more authoritative and whacked them with the lines hoping to scare them with the noise, but they were aware that a wimp was in control. I just didn't have the authority, and I couldn't fool them. They knew it and took advantage of it by only putting forth half the effort and obedience.

There never was one big magic moment that "gave" me control, but I kept at it and it did come. No matter how tired I got, how scary a turn was, or heavy the load, we hauled. My confidence went up a little each morning and the horses' independence grew less. And like a slowly healing wound or a headache, I never felt the actual moment the problem left, but I sure knew when it was gone. At last I was master of the team.

I changed, they didn't. I gained the needed confidence. The secret was keeping the reins of responsibility firm in my hands.

It's not "how many" flies that matters
But where they light and how they bite

Barnyards have their "swells" and smells, all part of the package. We just lived with them and got used to them. One of the harder things to get used to, however, was the tireless fly.

Barnyards always have flies; they love animals and any kind of animal "fallout" such as milk or manure. If you leave anything out, they'll find it, and contaminate it, too. On the farm there were flies of all kinds, including houseflies to spread diseases and pollute, deerflies to bedevil you, and horseflies to really take a bite out of you, gadflies and stable flies, and more. Business has its flies, too, thousands of them, buzzing, irritating, and sometimes lighting on you. If you spend all your time swinging at and swatting them, watching for and worrying about them, you'll never get any real work done. Flies, in business as in the barnyard, just come with the territory. Some of my least favorite but never go away flies, are whiners, complainers, threateners, competitors, cranky customers, recessions, some salespeople, and junk mail. Things like this buzzing in and around my head are just part of the package. Like the farm flies I learned to ignore, I just bend my back and keep on working. And if any light and bite I slap 'em—then, not before.

It also helps to remember the fly rule we had on the farm: Clean up everything immediately and keep it covered, and no matter how many flies there are, it won't matter. This principle of prevention has saved me hundreds of times in business from the kind of people who

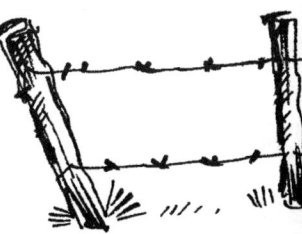

buzz around and snoop in your stuff. I leave nothing out on my desk or anywhere. When I'm finished with something, I file it away or pack it up and take it with me.

Teamwork!

The animals were really vulnerable in fly season, and as flies attacked their noses, ears, eyes, back, legs, and any open sores, they would often bolt and stampede. I've seen animals go crazy and knock sections of corral over, fighting flies.

Always compassionate to animals, Dad sent me and my brother to paint repellent oil in and around the animals' ears, and they never fought us at all, somehow knowing this was relief. We also put up oilers at all our animals' rubbing posts, so the animals could just rub on them and oil themselves. The wild animals and some neighbors' animals, however, just had to suffer the consequences of the pests. I must have only been nine or ten when we drove past some neighbor's horses grouped together on a hot August day—prime fly time. They were switching their tails vigorously, kicking, twitching their skin, shaking their heads—anything to keep the flies away. "Look," Dad said, slowing up and pointing, "at the difference between horses that take care of each other and go it on their own." This illustration is what I saw:

In business we have some really pesky flies, too, from the houseflies of local government to the deerflies of do-gooder organizations to the horseflies and gadflies of the IRS.

If and when we businesspeople (owners and workers) start taking care of each other instead of suing, coercing, undercutting, gouging, rule and loophole exploiting, blowing the whistle on, nitpicking, ganging up on, and taking advantage of each other, we'll eliminate many of those bureaucratic flies. They are attracted to and feed on our inability to work together in harmony and mutual respect. And as Dad pointed out—even horses' butts are lovable when they work as a team!

Working "with" people isn't a natural, automatic act—jealousy, selfishness, pettiness, and vanity all run deeper in our conduct than cooperation. "Me" and "mine" are some of the first words we learn when we're small and helpless and they're hard words to get rid of when we mature. If those words (ME/MINE) are the center of your life at home and in the workplace, you'll have a tough time when it comes to teamwork.

Move fast, and you won't get stung

"Slow down," "Slow down," "Slow down," always comes from slow people, and I find it strange that for the first twenty years of my life everyone encouraged or required me to speed up or hustle, and for the last twenty all the advice has been about slowing down. If you seriously intend to survive in business and enjoy it, I'd suggest you stick with the theme of the first twenty. Slow pays low dividends and slow is dull, if not downright boring. I've noticed that almost everyone will accept average or slow until they get up to speed, and then that's what they really want.

I trace most of my hustle back to the barnyard—for sure farmers aren't the slow, drawling dudes many people imagine them as. We lived near a marsh so there were lots of mosquitoes, and they were so big that after they ate the horse, they pitched the horseshoes to see who got the harnesses. We had no repellent in those days, so the only defense was to move so fast they couldn't light on you, and sweat so much they didn't want to. If you stopped to snack or visit they'd swarm you, so breaks just weren't worth it. This really ingrained some lifelong good work habits.

You'll notice that business has lots of mosquitoes too, people after you to sting you, irritate you, and suck blood out of you. The more

successful you are the more they gather, and they all want a bite. If I just sit at my desk all day they all find me and I spend all my energy dodging them or swatting and swinging away at them. By the end of the day I'm exhausted, but I've accomplished little. If, on the other hand, I'm up and running and doing all day, deeply engaged in a good cause and on the move constantly, I can just contact anyone who really needs me. I get lots done and feel a lot better at the end of the day.

The barnyard rule of survival was a good one to learn and practice forever: *Move fast and you won't get stung.*

Cows can get fat on grass

One afternoon not long ago, one of my friends, who was fighting a weight problem, said he couldn't understand why he seemed to be getting heavier, when all he was eating was salad. Without even thinking I remarked back, "Well, cows can get fat on grass."

It's easy to fall for the idea that if something is good for us we can't get enough of it. This is nothing less than a dangerous doctrine, in business or anything. Rest, sleep, play, milk, and whole-grain products are good for us, but an excess of them can ruin us just as effectively as something bad or evil. A field of clover is great for cows, ideal even, but if they overeat in it, there can be grim consequences (see p. 83). Toys are nice for kids, too, but give them too many of even the high-class educational kind and they become restless, possessive, and unhappy. Likewise vacations, days off, and breaks were introduced into the business world to give us a break in monotony and routine, recharge and refresh us and help us literally re-create our spirit and body. When someone's whole goal and thrust, in life or business, becomes "time off" and recreation, however, it really shows on the bottom line.

Fat is no better for business than it is for the body. On the farm, fat animals make poor workers and breeders as well as poor meat, and just like fat humans, they're far more susceptible to diseases and other health hazards. And employees that are either physically fat or too fixated on the "fat" of free time and easy money are gradually reduced to near worthlessness.

Few animals can handle a self-feeder, those devices that automatically drop more grain or whatever in the tray when some is eaten. With a self-feeder plenty (or you might say too much) is available all the time. A horse or a cow and many other animals will eat and eat and eat at one of these until they founder and die. They can't handle unlimited access, and neither can most of us.

So many people in business today are convinced that they can't get enough money, and as a result we have hundreds of thousands of non-producing "executives" and other professionals, all kinds of overpaid people. They know it and others know it, and still they will forever press for bigger salaries.

> Guess what animal never overeats and never gets fat at a self-feeder? The pig! Now that tells you something!

A big national company proposed moving to our town once, and the Chamber of Commerce and all the citizens were ecstatic about it: The thought of all those new jobs, all that new tax income, and the impetus this would bring would surely lend to other new development. It went through and the company did build their new headquarters, and paid a goodly amount more than the current going wage to the people

they hired. Soon that wasn't enough, and they were hit for more, and they paid it. Now there were demands for a covered parking facility, babysitting services, paid personal leave, and all kinds of other perks not necessarily the responsibility of the company, and they got them. This constant nibbling continued, until one day the company announced they were closing down and moving away to operate in a more economical locale. They simply couldn't produce the product here at a competitive price anymore. The whole town was suddenly up in arms criticizing the company, when it was locals that had caused the cost problems.

I remember well when I went through the "too much" stage back on the farm as a teenager. I was playing the guitar then and wanted to practice round the clock and forget about my chores and schoolwork. I was in love for the first time, too, and wanted to be with her 24 hours a day. I liked to play baseball as well (and had my eye on the big leagues), so I wanted plenty of time to play ball, too. My folks would say, "But Don, there can be too much of even a good thing," and boy, does that make sense now in business.

Leaning is losing

All business failures seem sudden, and all bring some broken hearts and broken families along with broken bank accounts and corporations. Because the final failure only takes a few days and is often so traumatic, the months and years that led up to it and really caused it are forgotten, so little is learned to prevent a repeat.

Walk into barnyards and look at the difference between successful and failing ones: it's an interesting evolution called *leaning*.

Seldom does anything in a barnyard—fence, stanchion, trough, gate, barn, or shed—ever get just suddenly knocked down and destroyed. What happens is that something gets a little off square and center from the weight and pressure of one or two-thousand pound animals leaning or pushing against it, high winds gusting against it, even the farmer running into it with the hay rake. Once something is tipped or tilted, it's off balance, and it's all too easy for it to be further tipped and tilted. Once it shows weakness, it's all too easy for it to get weaker. Incline just seems to accelerate decline. Yet in business, as in life, when something is slipping, we like the animals will just keep on using it as if it were still straight and strong. On farms that have failed, just look around and see how many things are leaning—the barn and the outbuildings lean, the doorways, the fenceposts, even the farm equipment and the outhouse leans. Go to a successful farm and everything is standing upright.

Things might lean for a long time before they go over, but go over they will.

You don't want any leaning in business, and by that I mean slipping from straight to a slanting compromise. Business, like the barnyard, is full of heavies who singly or in groups or herds will push and pressure you unmercifully. Giving a bit to release the strain is more comfortable than maintaining an erect stand. But once you tip, even a little, it's a red flag to the biggest bulls and bullies. Now they know you can and will come down. So even the slightest incline starts you on the path to decline. The final fall gets all the attention, but the real culprit is that gradual lean. This applies to business relationships as well as contracts, agreements, assignments, schedules and manufacturing specifications—it's that slight but ever increasing deviation away from what is straight and true.

This doesn't mean go make a prop for all your ailing, failing situations or structures. We too often just rig up props for our leans. Note as you go by the failing farm, how instead of actually repairing or restraightening anything, the farmer will "troubleshoot" with a temporary support. This keeps it from falling right then (and maybe for a while), but it doesn't deal with the problem. The unit is still crooked! Businesses spend a lot of time and money every day propping up all their leaners with legal maneuvers, gloss-over excuses, leaves of absence, little changes, etc.

Get the slant? *When something leans, something is wrong. Fix it!*

"Don't let 'em lie down..."

Logic? Proverb? Old wives' tale? I still don't know—but I heard it often enough in the barnyard to practice it beneficially in business.

On the farm if we had an animal acting strange or sick we worked to keep it up and moving, walking. If we could manage to keep them on their feet, they seldom died. But once they lay down, they seldom got up again.

Anything down, in barnyard or business, seems to beckon the buzzards and draw flies. It encourages people to give up and puts them in a good position to get stepped on. Nursing a downed critter or employee back to health always ends up a real outpouring of time, money, and emotion—IF you can ever raise or restore them. Things are heavier when they're down, too, so a good code of business here is: Don't let 'em lie down—your debtors, your crews, your prospective customers, or your sales force. People or deals kept "on their feet" (even standing immobile) are easier to heal. It's a lot easier than trying to restand them.

The toughest discipline

In the barnyard you learn plenty of hard lessons about life and death. Not only are many animals' lives shorter than ours, but they have their share of reverses and injuries and often no hospital or health plan. When a horse broke its leg, we all remember from the westerns, often the only alternative was to destroy it—a tough assignment on a loyal friend. It took me a long time to understand how killing could ever be kind. Emotions notwithstanding, it was the rule of the ranch: If the vet couldn't fix an animal then we had to deal with it. The longer we let it go, the more the animal suffered.

In business we have a similar problem with those who've become unproductive because of physical or emotional injury, or a drug or alcohol habit, or the like. We do have to deal with it to prevent a lot of suffering on both sides. I've seen plenty of healthy employees for that matter who have "died" on the job—they hate everything and everyone around them, they're thoroughly bored and miserable and make everyone around them miserable. But they hang on to suffer and complain. Taking care of situations like these—firing someone, or giving them that ultimatum—is often one of the hardest things we ever have to do. But if you don't have the guts or compassion to do it you'll never be much of a businessperson.

Never take new gates for granted

Anything new or different is hard to sell in business, or anywhere else. Any growing business will sooner or later call for some shifting of location or assignment, or entry into new areas. But even smart, seasoned people will balk at and resist even a good change.

I remember once back on the ranch we bought a bull who'd been kept in a single place all his life. In his old home pasture he went from West to East to eat, and now he had to go from East to West. At first he wore himself out going down the fenceline trying to go West to East. It took two weeks of work with him, walking after him in the rain and prodding him back the right way, showing him the new location of the food, before he got the idea and adjusted to it.

Another time, we changed the location of the gate on a long stretch of fence. It was kind of like using only one car door all the time and then having it welded shut and then using only the other. We herded the cows to the fence and they all bunched up at the place where the old gate had been, despite the fact that fifty-feet away was a wide open twenty-foot gate with plenty of fresh green grass on the other side. Do you think those stubborn critters could see that? Nope, they just crowded up to the old gate, milled, and mooed. They were there for hours before one or two of them gingerly walked up to the new gate, stopped, looked around hard, and finally eased through. Others did follow then, but some old diehards stood by the old gate place all night, mooing and starving.

You can put in a nice big "new gate" for humans, too, and still many will refuse to use it, and will moo by the gate of the old policy for years. So do prepare them. Don't expect them to automatically be responsive to changes in procedure or machinery. It always looks so easy to the herder (boss)—why those we are trying to relocate can't see it is beyond us. No matter how attractive the incentive on the other side, if we close in on, pressure, or squeeze them, they become totally defensive and will bolt, dive into the fence, or run for their lives.

Remember that even animals are very suspicious of a new opening at first. You have to make them aware of it and just give them some time. It is the nature of man or beast when pushed to push back, and to yield when you allow them a little time and space. Once one of them goes through, usually others will follow. People or animals, you do have to make it clear (like by banging the feed bucket to get a calf's attention, leading one of the cows through the new opening, or giving them a taste of the timothy on the other side) that what you have

in mind involves something good and desirable. Everyone cooperates better when they're convinced there's something in it for them. (The only catch here is to make sure the gate or door is really open.)

Control by feel

You can get so good at something you know by feel, or even the slightest sound, whether things are going right or wrong. I learned this running farm equipment, especially the baler. The tractor that pulls the baler is noisy enough, but the baler has noisy moving parts all over. Between the clanging racing of the pickup bar, the screaming of the feed auger, the whine of the power takeoff unit, and the deafening pounding of the plunger that packs the hay into bales, you can hardly hear yourself think. Yet on the back of the baler is a quiet knotter that ties the twine around the bales. It's almost noiseless, yet amidst all of the racket of baling, when the knotter mis-tied, I knew it. That is as amazing as a mother of six, who has her own children and three others playing and running all over the house, and yet in one second, if something is not right in all of that chaos, the mother detects it, and can intercept it.

I got that way with business, too. I never kept the books or worked on them, but could walk into the office any time and have my accounting department read me either the names of the payables and receivables I could name the amount, or vice versa, through dozens of pages. The bookkeeper was astounded—though he worked with those numbers all day, he couldn't do that. It was no miracle at all—any one of you could do it, too, if it was your responsibility to answer for all that. It's amazing, the math skill you acquire with ownership. Often you don't have to go onto a job site to find a problem. There was in our Vegas operation once, for instance, excessive supply costs for the amount of floor space being cleaned. No accountant could catch it because they look only at the accuracy of invoices and dates. Field people (which all business executives should remain) can sniff it out by scanning the books—there is a problem here! And sure enough, there was. An addicted manager was buying supplies and selling them off a tailgate at a flea market to support his drug habit. I mean how could one use 55 gallons of wax remover ($580) to strip a single floor (a $150 job)?

Controlling by feel assumes you know exactly how the baler—or your business—operates, so you can detect anything that deviates from the complicated music of the machinery. A clang or a clatter in the tone of a client or creditor, for instance, warrants a quick followup to see exactly what the problem is. Many times I've detected something slightly off key with one or the other, and quickly turned my attention to it, just in time to keep it a solvable problem rather than a crisis. This kind of experience and seasoning in the business proves useful in teaching later and surviving always.

You swing more weight standing

The first time I ever took a load of cattle to the sale in a truck, it was snowing and the roads were quickly getting slippery. I'd grown up driving icy roads and with the weight of several cows in back traction seemed guaranteed. But a standing cow is top heavy, and when they all shifted position on a turn, it was like having three thousand pounds on the end of a stick. It was one of my scariest moments ever at the wheel; I had absolutely zero control over that truck.

When I got home and told Dad how the cows had moved me all over the road, he said, "A standing cow swings a lot of weight." The same is true of much of the work you do on a farm—lifting, chopping wood, swinging a pick or sledgehammer—you can do it better if you put the strength of your legs into it.

In business standing carries the weight, too, in more ways than one. The Native Americans sat on the ground to bargain, and many people today do business sitting at tables or on bar stools, but I'm convinced that standing is the best position to be in in business, the best way to get most jobs done, even in meetings. When you're dealing or communicating, there is great physical and psychological advantage to being on your feet and not behind anything. There's a reason for those expressions "stand up and fight," "stand up and be counted," and "what I stand for…." We think better on our feet than on our fannies, we're more alert and ready for action (and less likely to fall asleep, too). And people are less likely to waste the time of a standing person, since you seem to be in the middle of something or on your way somewhere.

Get up when someone approaches you, and sit down only after they do. Standing, you're anyone's equal and you're in control.

West Forty

The reality of risk

In the course of one long interview, I hired a new manager, and as I ended our conversation I mentioned that being a leader in any area of business required some risk. He reached over, clasped his wife's hand firmly, leaned toward me, and said in the most earnest voice imaginable:

"Mr. Aslett, as long as we can pay our bills and eat, I'm willing to risk anything."

I leaned back at him and said, "Sir, that isn't risk, that's what everybody wants to do. When you possibly *can't* pay your bills and eat—that's risk."

Everyone these days wants a guarantee or warranty of success before they start out in business, and it just isn't there. What there is, starting or running a business, is excitement, challenge, independence, and always RISK. If you can't live with it or even thrive on it, I'd be cautious about ever going into your own business, or working your way too far up in someone else's.

Again I credit the barnyard, for "Risk Acclimatization 101." I said earlier that farming isn't a gamble, but it does come with risk; more risks than most businesses, so your best planning may never materialize. It may not rain, it may rain too much, you may be hit by hail, insects, birds, or problem animals. Or the crop may turn out perfect and so does everyone else's, so the bottom drops out of the market.

When I had no money I didn't think about risk, but after that nice profit I made on my pigs I had $400 in the bank (drawing a nice 2.5 percent interest). We were at a sale and Dad nudged me and said, "Why don't you buy those little heifers? They only cost $400 and will be worth $800 when they're grown." As they got closer to the sale ring I thought about my $400 sitting safely in the bank and finally I nudged Dad back and said, "What if they die?" Without a pause Dad said, "What if they don't?"

That summarizes the "Doctrine of Risk" in business. I bought them, and they didn't die. If they had, I'd have lived with it and kept going. Cultivating a "What if they don't die?" attitude instead of being unable to see beyond "What if they do?" is a real key to success in business. In other words, the simple willingness to take a risk.

Going without makes good folks

We've all heard the expression "dirt poor farmers." But you probably know as well as I do that no one who owns any dirt is poor. This judgment "dirt poor" is usually based on the absence of luxuries, not lack of necessities. And in the long run of life and business it's the necessities that bless, enrich, and sustain. And it's the *luxuries* that bring on the "poor."

I always feel a fondness for old farmers when they relate hard times, as I've found in business that those times are generally the most valuable!

"We didn't have much, but we had food and each other. We made our own games and entertainment, even our own clothes. We cared for each other—family and community."

"You had to learn to manage for the long dry spells. To get by, you had to live with what you had, no extras. We conserved wherever we could, and didn't waste anything. We never bought a new tool or piece of equipment until we knew exactly where the money for it was coming from. During the expansionary era in farming (right before the big bust), even banks would encourage you to borrow more than you needed. It's really hard to pay it back if you do that, and we never did. I guess you'd say we learned to live within our means, while working to improve our means."

What did those "dirt poor" farmers have? They had fresh fruits and vegetables not doused with all kinds of chemicals, well or spring water, fresh milk, butter, and meat from their own animals, low taxes, high hopes and horizons, lots of skills, a close family, good health, few fineries to store and worry about, and plenty of privacy and trust—we on the ranch couldn't even spell the word "lawyer!" "Dirt poor" starts sounding pretty good, doesn't it?

"Well off" today is actually a pretty sad situation. We're too busy to have each other, our entertainment is mostly second-hand and expensive, and we live drugged, taxed, and regulated to the max. A tiny lot-size piece of dirt surrounded by hot pavement now can easily cost $80,000 (that could have bought a whole community in "dirt poor farmer" days).

I got to live through some "going without" time myself in the 40's and in perspective now I see that it was the richest, most rewarding time of my years. Going without and getting by with less, allows time and space to live and love instead of racing for a more luxurious rat trap.

Barnyard consultants

It's probably a toss-up between the "hick farmer" and the "city slicker" as to who pokes the most fun at the other. We found it refreshing, even delightful, to have our town cousins come to the farm and watch them learn country ways. Some of our farm visitors were

"professionals," however—impressively educated representatives of the County Extension Office, the Bureau of Land Management, the Agricultural Testing Service, etc., and of course the veterinarian.

These folks always had well-ironed clothes and little pads and rows of pens in their shirt pockets, lettered vehicles, and thick official briefcases. Many of them didn't have near Dad's net worth, but they always strutted cockily onto the place, with plenty of wise words of advice as to how we could do our jobs better. Granted they were some help, but never to the degree they thought they were. The same was true of most of the bankers who came out and told farmers how to make and manage money. We treated them all cordially and always cooperated, but farmers were never too impressed by people who took hour-and-a-half lunches and quit work at 4:00 P.M. so they could make it back to the office and home by 5:00 P.M.

I remember one morning when two handsome khaki-suited fellows rolled into the yard in a new pickup, the metal rigging of their truck holding transits and markers. Politely addressing Dad they said, "Mr. Aslett, we're from the state Bureau of Land Management, and we'd like to run some gradient levels on yours and your neighbor's ranch to help you consider better drainage and soil conservation measures."

"Help yourself," Dad said, pointing to the road and gates to the area he knew they'd be most interested in. I was pretty awed by their instruments and the amount of writing and talking they did. They surveyed for two days and after they packed up to leave, they pulled through the barnyard to thank Dad. "What did you find out?" he asked them.

One of them unfolded a mass of coordinate paper and said, "Well, Mr. Aslett, the fall on the two flat pieces is seven feet, meaning we can do some routing…" Dad interrupted by slapping the side of the pickup and pointed to one of the fields and said, "Why you dummies, I can see with my naked eye that isn't a more than (he squinted) two foot five or six inch drop." I was as shocked as they were by Dad's presumption, but they just mumbled and said they'd be back to shoot it again tomorrow. And they did, and it was exactly two feet, four-and-three-quarters-inches! They were amazed and drove off like two beaten pups. Dad had been a grade foreman for a large construction company, and had built overpasses and mile-long airport runways, etc.—he had a superb eye for grade. I thought it was a little unfair that he never told them!

Barnyard experiences like these taught me well that the outside expert indeed has an outside view. He or she may have suggestions or "answers," but only you have full responsibility and accountability (and often, the cure!). We saw and heard lots of soil test and crop examiners, but it was usually the old successful farmer who brought up the yields. My early experience with city slickers and official experts of all kinds helped me later in business to deal wisely with all the "outsiders" pushing to be your agent, counselor, analyst, representative, etc. (for a percentage, of course).

If you can see all the wheels, you know what's going on

While I was going to college, my wife and I lived in town across the street from an elderly couple who went to Arizona every winter. The only bad part about the trip was the return, when the husband had to back their trailer into a long, narrow storage shed. It got to be a yearly

event of sorts and it took him hours, sweating, swearing, scraping the walls, and yelling at his wife for making him nervous by watching.

The couple loved my wife and she looked out for them, so one afternoon, the agony of the previous year still fresh in her mind, she came running in and said, "Don, the Collees are back. Would you go back their trailer in?"

We ran across the street and welcomed them home, and I offered to back the trailer. Proud as he was, the husband only hesitated a minute (a crowd was gathering) and then said, "Sure," and handed me the keys. In one try and a total of three minutes, I backed the trailer precisely into its slot. Everyone, including my wife, was amazed, but to me backing is as easy as driving forward. After the cheers, handshakes, and an almost tearful thank-you from Mrs. Collee for sparing them the annual homecoming anguish, I reflected back to where I learned to handle trailers, in the barnyard.

The reason it was so clear and simple on the farm, was that our tractors and trailers didn't have fenders, so you could see all the wheels. Once you can see not only the trailer but the angle of all the wheels, it only takes about two seconds to figure out the coordination between them. Anyone can do it, and when you're guiding a business it's the same. The power to guide and steer things is largely with "the big wheels" or executives. If they are covered, hidden, or out of sight you can't watch them. You have to navigate by feel and when the business starts to veer or swerve it's too late.

Executives often think they shouldn't be accountable like the rest of us, but in fact because their jobs are more critical they should be *more* accountable. Their doings and dealings should be out in plain view—every move, every expense and expenditure, every everything—because they affect your entire operation just like those tires. The whole tractor, the whole trailer, the whole bottom line moves in the direction those big wheels turn them.

If you don't tie in your bales, your stack will fall over

Those pretty bales of hay you see decorating so many farm fields are essential to the business of farming, and they end up in the barnyard. Keeping the hay in good condition once it's there is just as important as keeping your assets safe and your people satisfied once you have them in your business. This isn't done by just getting them there

and allotting them a spot. Hay or helpers, how you place and take care of them makes all the difference in how long they last.

Business looks so easy sometimes—just pick a place, hire some people, and get on with it. Ninety percent of businesses that just pile people up like this topple, like a poorly stacked haystack. Follow me to the barnyard to see why.

The square bales that most hay was put up into when I was young were transported from the field by the truck or wagon load, and when they got to the barnyard they were arranged into a giant pile called a stack. Exactly how you placed the bales in that pile was critical. My brother and I, first with a horse and wagon and later with a tractor in overdrive, would haul 1,000 bales a day and then stack them by hand. Our speed of assembling them often exceeded our skill at stacking them (which when done correctly, is called "tieing in").

In our earliest years we worked with Dad, who expertly lapped and laced one bale to complement another, so that each new line of bales was tied securely to the last line, and to the whole of the stack. Dad finally turned the construction of the whole main feedlot stack over to us, marking out a thirty-by-fifty-foot section of ground for us to erect our first stack. It seemed so easy on the lower levels that we started taking a few shortcuts in our bale stacking. We reached the thirteenth layer, full height, and were still doing fine. Our operation was looking good overall, when suddenly we noticed a slight crack in our beautiful stack. That little separation grew daily, from two inches, to five inches, to eight inches and twelve inches, and then one day a whole side of the stack just silently peeled off, clean as a slab of cut carrot cake. It sure left a big gap.

It took a couple more stacks before we finally learned how to hold our structure intact. In the barnyard or business, you just can't stand a bunch of bales or people or projects side by side and expect them to mold themselves into a single strong unit. There has to be interlocking at every level, not just the top or just the middle or just the bottom. Otherwise any little fracture line that develops will shear through your whole structure.

Dumb animals? Don't you believe it!

One of our large telephone building cleaning contracts was run by an elderly, sincere, hardworking, kind of slow and deliberate fellow, who frustrated the big executive boss of the telephone company at times. One day when I was in a review meeting with this executive, he slapped the cleaning specifications on his desk in disgust and said, "Damn it, Don, that manager of yours is dumber than six head of sheep."

I chuckled about that comment for weeks; it really struck me funny. But, working with my manager you couldn't help but love him. He'd die for me or the executive in question and just because a person acts like a sheep once in a while doesn't mean he's dumb. I've never tolerated anyone treating my crew or staff as "dumb." It's been a real key to my business success and I learned it (you guessed it) in the barnyard.

No animal is dumb, even sheep and chickens. They do dumb things but... don't we? Even with all our education we do things that are so dumb we can't believe it, and then we do even dumber things like lie about it. I think every big boss of any company or corporation should be required to put in a two-year internship (before they take any of those theory-packed 101 classes—sociology, psychology, behavioral science) with a herd of animals in a barnyard. If and when you are skilled enough to handle these well, then you would qualify for the classroom or conference room.

Animals not only recognize us, they react to our tone of voice, they know when we're afraid or angry, they know when we're going to hurt them. And they make us look and listen; a skill few businesspeople ever achieve. They have instincts, keen senses, and good sense we

don't even have—you learn gradually in the barnyard that animals aren't dumb and you don't treat them that way.

Being a janitor I can tell you there are plenty of people in business who treat others as dumb, especially those tabbed as subordinates. One waitress described it perfectly, "I'm not only human, I'm smart and hard working… and they treat me like a fixture." One of our professional cleaners, a lovely intelligent mother of four, was cleaning a men's restroom a while ago and some big wheel walked past the "Closed for Cleanup" sign and used the urinal right next to her. This was exactly the same as saying, "You don't exist, dummy."

I've cleaned areas filled with businesspeople (with ties and blouses brighter than they are) who never speak to me or even acknowledge my presence. I'm as well educated as any of them and I could buy and sell the whole room of them, but I get treated "dumb." People—regardless of their age, education, or national origin—are all a precious and valuable part of your operation. You need to see them as equals, not underlings, and learn to handle them instead of ruling them. If you can't learn and practice this in business, you're your own biggest liability.

(P. S. That big executive I mentioned earlier died at the age of 46 from the results of smoking and being overweight. No animal is that dumb!)

Culling is continual

The barnyard and the fields behind it practiced a law described in earlier days as separating the wheat from the tares. In other words, that process called "culling." It's always needed, for no matter how purely planted, well bred, carefully tended or stored, how well irrigated or sprayed a crop or anything else is, corruption always occurs. Weeds appear in the most weed-free fields. Runts come in the best of litters, rot develops in the cleanest bin, disease can strike the best tree, and weak seedlings come up out of the best furrow. All of the apples and all of the eggs will never be Grade A.

These same things happen in the best-run businesses. Discouragement and disloyalty can emerge at the peak of profits. The twenty-year honest earner can become dishonest, your most saintly clerk can become the most surly. Agreements can be bent and broken. No success is ever final—it has to be tended, tested, graded, and continually culled. We have to be ever ready to identify the negatives and remove them to allow the best-quality contenders to carry on and prosper.

On the farm we sorted and separated and singled out the spoiled, the second-rate, and the spoilers from the growing, living, and the stored, and we did it often. Tireless culling in business, likewise, will have a bigger effect on yield than anything else.

Build your team before you need it

On the ranch, in the barnyard, it was called herd building. We did it because of a basic truth that applies to all operations: No matter how good things are going, how up the market is, how much money you are making, no matter how prime the crops or the critters are at any given time, IT WON'T LAST forever on its own. Things grow old and wear down and wear out—not just cows and cherry trees but people (clients, customers, contacts, key employees). Someday the yielding will decrease and cease and replacement will be mandatory. Call it change or attrition if you wish, this is one of the biggest success or failure points in all business, barnyard or boardroom. For if a replacement has been planned on, prepared, tabbed and groomed for a slot that suddenly needs filling, the transition is smooth and efficient, not stressful, and generally inexpensive.

Herd building is a practice all good farmers, ranchers, and dairymen have engraved solidly in their practice, because they know that the best cow or sow in the world can get sick or die and that the best orchard or berry patch will someday quit bearing. They never wait till the day of reckoning—they keep those grafts and seedlings coming and those prime new calves breeding toward the day their high performers retire on them. Good baseball teams do this, too. Even while they're at the top of the league standing, they're buying and building and working with young ballplayers daily, knowing full well that someday their best slugger will get sluggish.

Twenty years of watching this constant selection and grooming of farm animals and fields and machinery to keep the abundance coming was one of the best lessons in business management I ever had. Be ready ahead!

A bad year doesn't necessarily mean a bad idea

Part of an education in business is not letting a couple of bad years give you bad information about a good crop. Just because the grass-

hoppers or frost ruin a yield it wasn't the crop's fault, nor necessarily a reason to quit growing it.

It seemed like a sound and logical idea to own my own janitor supply company along with my own janitorial service, for instance. Why not buy cleaning chemicals and equipment from myself and also sell it to others? My idea was right on for the little company I called Micro Clean Supply. I planted well—established purchase and product lines, printed business cards and stationery—but didn't have the laborers (or the time myself) to tend and harvest. So I had a bad year, a crop flop. The business died but the idea didn't.

Six years later, the climate looked better. We were a more efficient, versatile organization with some depth. We did some research and started another entity we called Varsity Supply, figuring we could now marshal enough volume to justify direct discount purchasing. However within a year we found ourselves in the same situation as before—it was a tagalong operation we hoped would just sort of run itself—and we experienced another drought, no fruit or harvest. The meager margin of supply savings involved wasn't worth the management effort, so back on the shelf it went. Time to quit farming? Not yet.

The third "planting" ten years later found fertile ground. In my first book, *Is There Life After Housework?* I not only explained how to clean like a professional, but included a little chart of the best tools and supplies home cleaners could use, directing them to a local janitorial supply store for the purchase. However there are not many janitorial-supply stores even in big towns and none in small towns—so letters from people trying to locate pro supplies poured in. Soon I was selling a few things and making $25 a day profit, then $50 (that's $1,500 worth of income a month for only a small investment in staff and space). So I printed up a primitive, one-page catalog and included one in each book sold. This gave us $300 a day in sales—a huge $3,000 a month income without going out of the office. My long-attempted supplies business was well launched without a startup cost. My "Cleaning Center" catalog now goes out to hundreds of thousands of people a year, and we have three retail stores with many more on the drawing board. And my cleaning products (including my own product line now) are sold by the millions on QVC, the premier TV home shopping channel.

Bottom line was sticking to a good crop. I had a few crop failures, but eventually reaped an exceptional harvest. A stumble or setback in barn or business isn't necessarily a sign to stop—just tighten your belt and flex your muscles and go for it again. A bad year doesn't always mean a bad idea.

The day of rest

All need it, the Creator commanded it, and we try to ignore it. After all, there's so much to do!

Even on the farm, where there are many more things (such as milking the cows and feeding the animals) that really do have to be done every single day, Mother always found a way for us to minimize, if not eliminate, Sunday work. We placed bales ahead on Saturday, overstocked feeders, and fixed water to run freely in the pasture instead of on the crops. So even at the busiest times we could manage something resembling a day of rest. (Mother never did manage to convince me, however, that machinery would always break down if you used it on Sunday.)

After six full days of business, businesses continue to fight for Sunday opening, afraid they might lose a dime if they don't exhaust the week completely. There are emergency situations that do have to be dealt with immediately, of course, and some businesses for which weekend trade is the main focus, but in general both barnyards and businesses run better with a day of relief.

Don't give up your stallions because they have a "mean streak"

Sometimes orneriness is actually a deep suppressed or unexpressed energy for good. This is as true of people as it is of animals, as illustrated by a true story Ron Hawks of Paul, Idaho, told me many years ago. It has had a profound effect on my toleration of rebellious kids and employees. It helped me realize that rebels, in the end, are often much more talented, willing, and even disciplined than all those content, docile, and cooperative folks.

A well-known judge had one of his champion mares bred by a world-famous stud. A nice colt resulted and was kept in a paddock corral. As he neared full size, now a healthy yearling, it was apparent to all that the young stallion was headstrong and disobedient. One afternoon the judge and several other dignitaries were touring the stable and stopped in front of this magnificent animal, who was in one of his mischievous moods. At such moments he would nip and bite and even lunge at people just to get attention.

On this particular day, the colt decided none of the stuffed-shirt senators were paying proper homage to him, so he reached over the fence and grabbed the collar of the closest man's suit coat firmly in his teeth. Then he shook the heck out of the coat—and the man, too—finally tearing that nice worsted entirely off. And away he ran, triumphantly flipping the coat around in the air.

The men, of course, drew back in horror and one of them said to the owner, "Judge, that animal is going to get you if you keep it. I'd get rid of it right now!"

The judge answered, " He certainly has been meaner than sin lately... maybe I will sell him."

"Man," another friend piped in, "He'll kill you for sure if you don't."

"Well," said the judge, "if I could just get my breeding fee out of him... [and he named a figure] I'd sell him."

As the horse continued to ricochet around with the senator's coat, a young corral hand (a true horseman who knew, loved, and understood horses) nearby said, "Judge, I'll be happy to pay you that for the horse."

The judge hesitated a second, with all his friends (especially the defrocked one) spouting encouragement. "Take it, take it!" And so the judge did.

The young man wrote out a check on the spot, then brought out a halter and tied the colt to his car to trot it down the road a couple miles to his neighbor's farm until he could come back to get it with a horse trailer.

Now this man knew the nature of horses at any age, and he knew that the temperament of a highbred horse is at its very worst in a young stud. That horse was thrilled to be outside the paddock and free at last, and after the two miles it was still frisky and snorting with glee. So the man decided to go on to the next house, closer still to his own farm, with this horse who was enjoying the exercise. Another six miles and the horse was even more turned on and raring to go. So on to the next, with the horse only gaining energy all the while, until the young horseman and horse had traveled the entire 47 miles home. When he turned the colt out into his pasture it ran, bucked, and leapt for another thirty minutes.

This colt, which he named Senator, became one of the finest trick horses in the country, a joy and beauty to behold. The young owner trained him to do all kinds of things. For example, if someone wanted a picture with the horse, the trainer commanded Senator to go over and sit down next to them and without fail the horse would quietly amble over and sit on its rump by a surprised poser. Senator could do math, too: "Senator, what's 5 + 6?" and the horse would paw eleven thumps on the ground. Turned loose in a rodeo arena, Senator would follow the most complicated directions of where to go and what to do, to the delight of the thousands of people in the stands. He was so magnificent, so obedient he had to be eliminated from competitions so the judges could give the rest of the entries a chance. He went on to sire hundreds of other foals and inspire hundreds of thousands of people in his life—all because one man understood that a "mean streak" doesn't have to mean a permanent black mark.

Ganging up

The "ganging up" principle is a familiar one on the farm. If you ran from one animal in the barnyard, they'd all join in the chase. Or one cousin would wrestle you down, another would yell "dogpile," and every kid in hearing distance would jump on you.

Ganging up can be seen in business, too. Just get yourself in a pinch or bind and all kinds of other things will crop up to inflict additional pressure. Getting yourself into a jam seems to mean automatic multiplication of your miseries, or an advertisement for more weight on you. Have a tax misunderstanding with one division of the government and they all flock to your ledgers. Have a setback and watch how many vultures start circling around.

The secret here is to stay on top. No one can dogpile you if they don't ever get you down. Never operate from a down, disabled, or under position (discouraged, behind, out of stock, ill tempered with someone, etc.). Business brings setbacks regardless of your expertise. You may, for example, be in a foul mood for a good reason, but opening shop with it is an invitation for everyone to step on rather than around you, and they will. You may not be able to prevent a problem, but don't operate with it, don't go into the game with an open wound. Fix it before you get near the gang, or they'll dogpile you.

Keeping out of the dogpile is much easier, cheaper, safer, and less traumatic than getting out once you're caught and buried. Keep in front, on top, and on time, and no one can gang up on you.

It isn't the breed, it's the individual

Agricultural people are pretty non-bigoted. On the farm in the old days you might hear an occasional smart remark about some immigrant group other than the one you came from, but we had real reinforcement of the truth working in front of our eyes every day. We had animals of every kind and color—black, white, brown, yellow, red, tan,

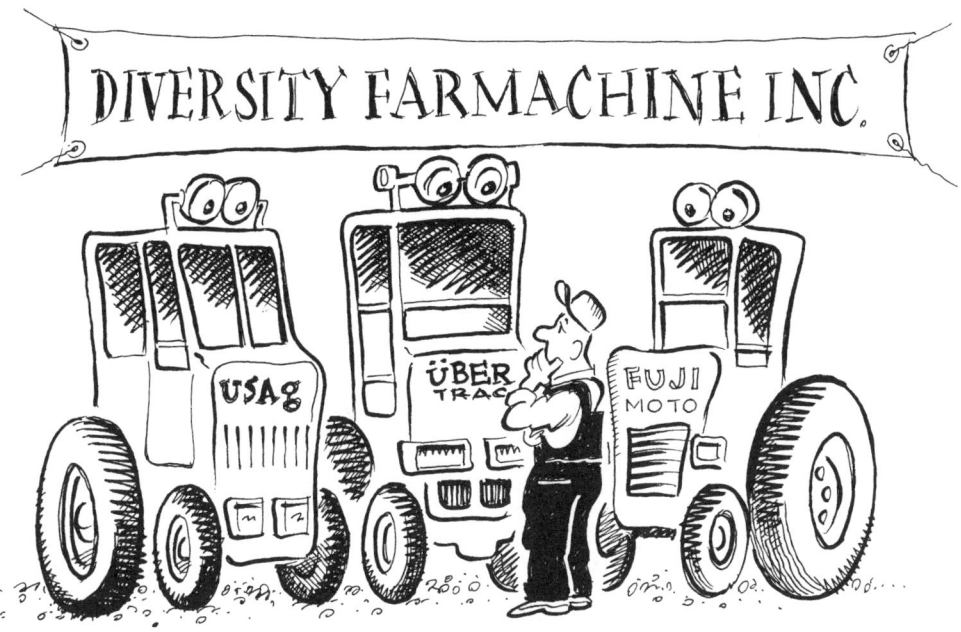

half breeds of all kinds, animals with long hair, short hair, long noses, short noses, male and female, and yes we had the handicapped: the lame, the blind, and the imperfectly formed.

Farmers don't judge a book by its cover; they judge things by output. They don't care if something is short, tall, fat, skinny, or ugly, as long as it does what it's supposed to do. They're not tied to any one type or brand of thing, to any one crop or variety of animal or make of machine. They don't care what country made the tractor if it does a better job. They've seen fields of big tall pretty corn and then a field of short stuff right beside it that outproduces the pretty field by bushels per acre. So we *had* to learn that color and race had little to do with relationships and results.

Farmers also know well, from keeping and working with animals, that it isn't the breed, it's the individual—every single cow, chicken, dog, cat, and piglet is as different from all the others as, yes, individual people are within a race or nationality. Every Pilgrim goose or Charolais cow or Nubian goat is an individual, a personality, with different and distinct habits, temperament, strong and weak points, etc.

And when it comes to equality of the sexes, farm women are anything but patronized sex objects. They've always been true partners

with their men, working hard right alongside them on a common venture, and sharing equally in the outcome.

On the farm, fortunately, we didn't have any do-gooder agencies hovering around, outlining separate corrals and special feed and treatment for this or that. If business, like the barnyard, could focus on net gain instead of hair nets and genetics, business could function more freely for everyone.

What's the #1 success word of business?

"Clean," of course!

I'm asked over and over in my television appearances and magazine interviews: To what do I credit my interest in "clean?" The answer is easy—the barnyard.

That might surprise you, since the most exposure many people these days get to a barnyard is to drive by on a humid day and smell it. This could and generally does give the impression that the barnyard is a dirty place. Barnyards also get a bum rap from expressions like "where were you raised, in a barn?" when you leave the door open.

But barnyards were the best boot camp for teaching cleanliness I've ever seen—the Army will tolerate a lot compared to a barnyard. You either kept things clean or you answered for your sloppiness. If you didn't pick something up as soon as it fell, you paid dearly for it. If you left it down, you ended up digging it out—it disappeared or was trampled on. Even as a young child I could see how much better my parents did because they always kept their tools and supplies clean and neat and contained, when so many of our neighbors and relatives were always losing things, and wasting time hunting or replacing them.

On the farm, it didn't take long to learn that clean paid off. If we gave animals a clean yard and environment, they kept themselves clean, which eliminated a lot of sickness and injury. Keeping the weeds cleaned up around the house and yard kept insects and rattlesnakes away and the cockleburs out of the animals, and a clean, shiny shovel was much easier to dig with than a dirty one. Everything that came out of the thresher or combine (beans, wheat, or peas) clean brought a higher price, and even the irrigation water ran three times better through clean ditches. Our equipment was kept clean so it always worked well, and our fields were kept clear of rocks and litter.

As a result, the barnyard was a place of fresh air and fresh feeling. Take the water trough for example. Cowboys might bathe in them, Clint Eastwood might shoot holes in them, but no self-respecting cow will drink out of one if it's dirty. (Yet humans will drink about anything that comes down the pipe.) People toss clutter and waste all over, but a pig would never do that. They go to one area of the pen to leave all their droppings, neatly.

When something is clean it looks and feels good—it's bright, beautiful, and functional. "Clean" is the number one success word of any business, starting with the place and grounds and extending to the ethics of the operation.

Foul language doesn't work (and no decent chicken would use it)

Profanity, cursing, and uncouth slang is so out of place everywhere—barnyard or business—it's really surprising that anyone with any degree of intelligence would use it. Because it just doesn't work.

I can remember plenty of "vivid" (more like livid) vocabulary in the barnyard when I was growing up. Hired men, truckers trying to load stubborn calves, and even a few of my uncles reeled out some of the most creatively presented cuss words imaginable. We kids weren't allowed to repeat any of these words—they were for adults only. We

couldn't help hearing them, though, because they generally carried all the way to the house, where even the womenfolks' ears were tinged.

Mother had her own way of retaliating here, of neutralizing this indecent exposure. She told us to observe carefully, to see if the cussing ever corrected or improved anything, or impressed anyone. We did, and it didn't. The cattle never loaded any differently, no matter how numerous or well-constructed the filthy phrases. No tool or machine that broke ever jumped up and healed itself, no matter how thoroughly it was cursed for breaking. No motor ever started easier or ran more smoothly because it was damned, and smashed fingers and stubbed toes didn't quit hurting. And we never did see anyone applaud or say, "Wow, that was a great string of words!" So, from Mother's masterful appraisal in the barnyard, I learned that swearing was a total waste of good emotion and personal prestige, not to mention risky (if a kid got caught swearing it was the old soap-in-the-mouth sentence).

Sailors and truck drivers have been singled out as some of the winners in the world series of wicked words, but many a sharp, clean office is cluttered today with this kind of vocabulary, from well-bred and educated lips. Women exercise their right to swear almost as much as men these days, too, so we probably hear overall more swearing in the course of a day than ever. Swearing is bad business in any business because:

1. You never know who you're offending or making uncomfortable with it, from clients to the CEO. Many people despise crudeness and won't deal with it or have it around them.
2. It's definitely poor manners, and poor manners lose customers, assignments, and sales.
3. It reduces people's confidence in you, and makes you look incompetent even when you're not.

Swearing should be left out of not only business and the barnyard, but out of our atmosphere and vocabulary entirely. There's nothing like working in a "word clean" environment.

New growth needs new ground

On the farm we learned early that if you want a bigger crop you have to break out every so often and plow new ground. Tending the same fields the same way will give you about the same yield, whereas expanding, adding acres and rich new soil increases yields. Be it profit or potatoes, the principle is the same.

New ground is necessary for new growth and this requires some nerve, faith and effort. You can call this breaking new ground, or simply plowing. It is really pioneering—clearing a place to plant new seeds.

There's always a crowd in the shade

When things get hot in business or the barnyard, everyone seeks relief and will fight to get to a sheltered area. With animals we called this "shading up." Animals will seek out a protected area, fight for a slot there, and then stay there until the heat is off before they go back to the business of grazing or galloping.

Shade may be nice and cool, but to me it's inactive and unappealing. The occupants of shade are always lazy and lethargic, and who wants to watch or work with anything just "shaded up," all minds and miracles at a dead stop? The shade isn't only crowded, it always has the most flies, the most manure, and the worst odor—and that should tell you something.

Too many business programs and policies seem to have swung toward actually aiming to attain shading up, hiding out from the main arena where you fight for goals and gains. The shade may be relaxing, but it's not where any business champion would choose to be. Winners let sweat keep them cool!

When the water freezes, you have to carry it

A water source in the barnyard is a luxury. In old barnyards you carried a little out from the house to clean off the cows' udders or to mix the calf feed, or you pumped it by hand for animals who guzzle gallons. Finally we had it piped to the barn with a faucet, so there was instant easy access to water. Of course after a while we didn't appreciate it very much… until it froze up.

First it froze at the spigot where a little heat or fire would get the fluid flowing again. But if it got cold enough and you got careless enough, the pipes would freeze down deep in the ground. Then you'd have to carry water in the bitter cold, in 5-gallon buckets that weighed forty pounds each. With each step you'd stagger back and forth, and the water that splashed and spilled froze on your Levied legs. It was pure misery—and unnecessary. Yet it seemed we'd always wait and let things go, let it freeze, and then have to resort to the hard way of getting the job done.

Finally, sick of carrying and facing up to the fact that the pipes weren't going to thaw by themselves, we'd devote a day to it. We either had to dig up the pipes and hook up a welding machine to heat them up, or build long fires on the ground over the pipes to drive the frost out. A great flood of relief followed the welcome gush of water, plus a vow to insulate the ground above the pipes or leave a drip to prevent another freezeup.

Good employees' loyalty is exactly like that barnyard water. Often we learn this the hard way, waiting until things freeze up before we give them any attention. Some people serve us like a water pipe. Any time we turn their faucet they're there, and it saves us from carrying a big heavy load. We get ungrateful fast and just expect it, in fact the quicker they respond, often the less sensitive we become to the source of it all. When we feel things start to get chilly we only worry a little because we're still getting water. Then when one frosty night they quit, we're stuck carrying the load, cooking the meal, cleaning the toilet, or waiting tables in our own place.

Waiting for a freezeup before pursuing preventive patterns is as foolish in the office, store, or café as it is on the farm. The cost to warm things up again, to get people "turned on" again, is always more than finding a match to start a fire. Frostbite does more than interrupt or delay the flow of work—it often breaks the pipes, and then you have to dig down and replace them. So if by chance you have some nippy, chilly situations coming on right now at work, I'd counsel you to warm things up immediately.

Too big, too bad

Believe it or not, about three quarters of all businesses fail, sooner or later, and that's a real heartbreak because in the end it's people who are hurt. And the dreams, savings, and sacrifices of a lifetime are often lost. Sincere, honest people lose everything they've got every day of the week, sometimes with agony and scars that never heal. So that little notice in the mail or newspaper, that announcement telling us some operation is defunct or "gone under" is not just a bunch of equipment up for auction, a building out of use. It's someone like you, me, our kids, our parents, or friends. When business failure comes it's seldom pleasant and anything you can do to discourage, prevent, or reverse it is sure worth learning.

I've never feared failure but man do I respect it. In the barnyard, a lot of the things we worked with—animals, machinery, vehicles, etc.—were bigger and stronger and faster than us. We were never allowed to forget that "Anything that can hurt you, will… if you let yourself get careless." And since failure or hurt so often come when we bite off more than we can chew, we were taught from the beginning not to take on anything beyond our capacity.

From the age of six onward we were encouraged to do plenty, and to tackle the big, even the seemingly impossible—but to be sure to divide it into manageable pieces first. Two trips to get a giant load of logs, for example, was a lot safer and in the long run faster than crowding and straining to get it in one. Things that were too big or heavy to control always broke the machinery or the person. Dad taught us to never underestimate the size of the rock, timber, cow, or gate we were trying to lift or move, because if you did you'd get squashed.

It's exactly the same in business. The fine line between expansion and overload is too often learned the hard way. People try to carry more than they can lift in terms of debt, time, equipment, or emotion, and they go down in defeat and despair.

There was one demonstration of this principle I never forgot. When I was a college freshman, my off-campus basement apartment was

in the home of the Smith family. One of their two children, Gary, an enthusiastic twelve-year-old, was my buddy. So much so that at the end of the year I invited him (a pure city slicker) out to the ranch for a couple of weeks. He'd been pretty pampered and protected, a status that ended quickly after he got there. Gary ate at least twenty things that he'd turned down for years. He slept in an unheated bunkhouse and got up at dawn. He drove a truck and a tractor (his mother nearly fainted), and at least 10,000 mosquitoes took their turn at him. He was a good kid and we had him Westernized pretty quick, but the old lesson of too big, too bad was yet to come.

One afternoon we were out at the corral working and Gary was perched on top of a six-foot-high fence rail, cowboy style, fiddling with a lariat. A herd of whiteface calves was strolling around inside, and some passed temptingly near him. "Can I lasso one of those cows?" he asked Dad. "You keep that rope away—those cows are bigger than they look!" And they were. They were yearlings, which meant they weighed an average of 370 pounds. They didn't look like much, but they were stronger and faster than a Volkswagen! Finally one of the calves ambled irresistibly close to the fence and Gary—and down went the lasso over the calf's head, a perfect toss. Gary quickly wrapped the end of that forty-foot rope around his waist and arm as tightly as a Cleopatra snake bracelet, and then braced himself atop the top rail. The lassoed yearling, now spooked, ran off at top speed. When the momentum hit the end of the rope, Gary did miraculously remain attached to his arm, but he flew straight out into the air till he hit the manure-frosted ground twenty-five feet from the fence. Then he was dragged all the way down the corral until the rope finally unwound. I now knew for sure I never wanted to lasso anything that would drag me where I didn't want to go, in business or anywhere else, and when Gary stood up, the consequences, how and where it would leave you, were mighty clear.

Do you kill the gophers...
...or later the stock with a broken leg?

One of the clearest lessons of the barnyard is that negatives have to be dealt with—*now*. The businesspeople who can't do this give business a bad name. When I was growing up, for example, the gophers and rockchucks didn't just eat a lot of crops, they left dangerous holes that grazing stock could easily break a leg in. Did you get the gophers, or wait and then have to shoot cattle and horses with broken legs?

In the 60s, likewise, rabbits almost took over some of the Western states. Thousand and thousands, full divisions of them, would attack and destroy crops. They could eat a whole haystack in an evening. So we either had to quit the business, let the cows starve to death, or kill the rabbits. We chose to kill the rabbits, and it earned us the international nickname of "bunny bashers." When there was a full moon my brothers and I would lay out on the stack with our .22's fixed with telescopic sights, and as the masses of rabbits migrated to our stacks, kill them. It was ugly but essential. You couldn't wait and hope for them to go away or wait another year to see if you could afford more hay. Yes, you had a heart but you couldn't yield to it if you wanted to survive.

The barnyard forces you to face issues like these in a way that many businesses don't. Those of us who own or run businesses often think we can wait for a better time to deal with a threat or a menace. If we have some exterminating to do, we don't want to have to do it because it's tough or unpleasant. We had to in the barnyard. You have to do it in business, too, if you don't want employees or subsidiaries stepping in the holes.

Tie it down

Sooner or later we all learn that anything hanging loose can hurt you. If you don't tie things down they'll blow out of the back of the truck; if you don't tie down the tarp it'll blow away; if your hat isn't tied down it'll blow off. And when it comes to dealing with your fellow humans, if you don't tie down a relationship or a plan or project it too will blow away. What should you use? Ropes will work loose.

The only tiedown in business, in fact in life, is the rope of commitment—learning to say I WILL and mean it. "I'll try..." "Maybe," "I'm working on it," "Later," "If..." "We'll see..." are poor and undepend-

able anchors. Only one really works and simplifies the whole business, and that is the ability to say I WILL. Commitment is the most effective tether for anything. It adds solid steel to our backbone and removes all the lazy bones. And it'll prevent things from blowing off, out, away, or all over. It's the smartest business move you'll ever make, a timely, "I will."

Read before you feed!

I remember one morning back on the ranch Dad telling me to take the fifty-pound bag of bone meal out in the shed and mix it into the pigs' self-feeder. So I packed that heavy brown bag of floury stuff out there and mixed it with the chopped hay and grain in the feeder. A week later Dad came striding into the house, "I thought I told you to mix that bone meal in the feeder!"

Rarely did I have the courage to stand up to my father outright, but I was sure of myself here so I puffed up and said, "I did."

"You didn't!"

"I did too!"

"You did not!"

By then we were both headed out to the shed to prove our points. Dad flung the door open and said, "What's that?" pointing to a brown sack, which when examined closely indeed said, "Bone Meal."

"I don't care, I still say I did...."

"You did not."

The argument was over later that day when Mother, who had purchased fifty pounds of plaster of paris for a church project, realized it was gone. I'd fed the pigs plaster of paris! So if any of you experienced a tougher than usual pork chop, now you know.

They say we get in trouble not reading the fine print, and that is true. But even when we don't read it we're usually aware of it, or worried about it. We can get into even bigger problems not reading the large print, those labels and warnings and headlines on cans and packages and bottles, tools and gauges and dipsticks, signposts and contracts. In the case I just described, of the pigs and the plaster of paris, I just saw the size, shape, and color of the sack, and grabbed it. Read the bold print and follow it and you'll seldom need to worry about all the fine print. The fine print is to observe the laws and regulations and copyrights, etc. The large print is for survival and operation. If you survive and operate the rest is easy.

The experts

I always liked watching real professionals work, to see just how good some people could get in their profession. It was easy to see at the ballfield or concert hall or even the used car lot. An expert can walk around a car once, not even kicking the tires, and tell you everything that's wrong with it. Some can just listen to it run and rock it, and know it better than some of the computer analysis machines they hook up.

Growing up with cattle, I always thought I was pretty good at judging and handling them. I'd been through the whole spectrum of feeding, branding, milking, herding, medicating, and butchering, and then one day I went with my father with some cattlemen (real cattlemen—old experienced buyers and ranchers). They were unloading several boxcars of yearlings from a train. Once the doors slid open, those penned-up animals poured out of the cars into the corrals for the buyers. My job was simply to count the critters, which I was having a hard time doing. One of the old sweat-brimmed sages told me with a twinkle in his eye not to try to count the bodies, but just count the legs and divide by four, which I did much to his delight. One batch I counted as 416—they roared with laughter and just quickly eyeballed the herd and said there were 380. There were 381 on final count—never did know how they did it but they were good.

Then came weight guessing. The six of them leaned over the corral and looked over the herd, and one said, "Well, gentlemen what do they weigh? For a steak dinner—losers pay." Most of us would be lucky to hit within fifty pounds guessing the weight of animals this size, but their guesses were 385, 387, 382, 388, 384 and the last guy said "Oh, they'll weigh a mite over 385 1/2." When the cattle were weighed they averaged 386 pounds, and the fellow whose guess came closest hit his fist on the corral pole in disgust and said, "Dang, I didn't figure the weight of the water!" (Several of the calves had fallen into a trough and jumped out). I ate a pretty humble hamburger as they ate steak.

In my business as a professional cleaner, being that good was my goal, and little by little I entered the league of that kind of expert. After many years I could almost tell the condition of a building (as well as the owner's attitude toward it) just from looking in the janitor closet. I could see a cleaning supplies purchase order for a college and know what they were doing right or wrong with their floors. I could tell by counting the mopstrings left on a floor who was bleach-

ing mops. I could appraise the time needed to clean a building and the cost of doing it in less than an hour and be right on the money. I could tell from the trash how efficient a place was. I didn't have to discover what the problems in cleaning a place would be; I knew them before I started the job.

When you eat, drink, sleep, and live your profession, it slowly becomes second nature. It doesn't take a brilliant mind as I once thought—just sticking with it and a passion for what you do.

Horns look bad, but it's the hooves you have to watch

Reading a hunting magazine once, I came to a page posing the question: "What is the most dangerous animal in the world?" All around the edges of a big chart were the ones that come immediately to mind—rhino, elephant, rattlesnake, grizzly, wolf, cougar, shark, and lion. But right in the middle was the uncontested leading life-snuffer—that barnyard biggie, the farm bull. None of the other more colorful and exotic creatures had anywhere close to the number of notches racked up on the doorjamb of the barn by the plain old ordinary bull. More interesting yet is the fact that the damage is seldom inflicted by those life-threatening looking weapons, the horns. Bulls seldom gore you to death—they tromp you to death. This was made clear to me by every grandpa, uncle, and cowboy back on the ranch. It's the weight a bull carries, 2,000 pounds or better, and their feet that do the dirty work on you. If you get in front of a bull, they'll toss you in the air; get under one and they'll make hamburger of you.

Likewise, in business we too often end up under the hooves, while watching and worrying about the horns. For example we are watching the immediate bottom line (the horns) instead of the goal line (the hooves) of the business. Or we focus on the style and cut of the new uniforms (the horns), instead of the contentment and loyalty of the crew (the hooves).

If you find yourself threatened by some of the animals you do business with, you might start using your hooves instead of always depending on your horns. Instead of standing there butting heads as too many horned executives do for position on a deal, use your hooves to trot away and find another one. Or make a new run at the objective. Remember, the horns can only go where the hooves decide. Hooves can kick and jump and dodge and push and pull and point and paw the earth and scare people into paying attention—even paying their bill!

A crop failure isn't a farm failure

Bad news is no stranger to the barnyard! I remember one fall when fifty-two of our small herd of feedlot Herefords were at 1000 pounds each, grain fattened and well qualified to be sold as "choice." The market was the highest it had been for quite a while and they were to be sold the day after tomorrow. All went as scheduled until I glanced in the corral and saw eight legs sticking up, a sad signal to us farm folk. We'd lost two of the herd to a freak bloat on third cutting hay—almost $900 gone! In other words, our profit, enough then to buy a tractor. Our bean crop also froze on the Fourth of July that year, and the two losses together were quite a blow to our efforts, cash flow, and ego. Walking out to the field we beheld devastation. Every plant was blackened and wilted to the ground. Our beautiful bean crop, our major source of income, gone. All our work, all that investment and expectation, wasted.

How sorry I felt for Dad, who had the burden of supporting all of us. I saw no tear or slumped shoulder, and heard no snarl, not even a choice curse or two. He just sadly surveyed the loss and then said, "Well, we better hustle, plow this under and plant—we still might get some kind of crop." And we did.

Failures like these on the farm were part of the package if you chose to pursue agriculture. Fires, frost, flood, disease, and accidents were all included in the "spilt milk" we weren't supposed to cry over. But setbacks hurt, and something "bombing" in any business can be a bust *if* you treat it as a defeat. Crop and herd failures weed out a lot of semi-committed farmers, just as a few bottom-line reverses pare out a lot of semi-committed businesspeople.

You don't abandon your body when you break an arm or smash your toe, and you don't dump a pursuit because something's gone defunct on you. Learning to plan in and compensate for the shortfalls is key to any kind of success. Those who quit and move on because of a failure or two have that pattern in all pursuits thereafter. Those who use the tears to germinate another stand enjoy some great harvests.

Mom's comment to Dad when the bad news of the two dead feeders came was, "Duane, let's be thankful death stayed in the barnyard." We didn't let things like this get in our house, head, or heart and so they really were just a crop failure, not a family or farm failure. Out of thousands of jobs and projects I've carefully planned in my corporate world, an occasional "crop failure" still occurs. The smart thing is to blend it in with the whole and roll on!

> **Don't take work woes home**
> The barn—workplace—can have a lot of reverses and often they don't stay at work (in the barn). We too often bring the ills and spillover of work home to stew over, or take out on spouse or children. Much family turmoil can be avoided if we follow Mother's counsel of being thankful, and letting some things, such as pressures, anger, injustice, and deadlines, stay in the barn.

Build bigger than you need right now

Another thing I learned on the ranch was to build capacity past the immediate need. In other words build the barn or corral bigger than you need it right now, make more room in the store or storeroom, more bedrooms in the house, because everything will grow and need more room. An eighteen-inch culvert is only a little bit larger than a fifteen-inch one, but it can carry a lot more water and is stronger and better able to handle occasional emergencies, as well.

Extra space is always welcome and a motivator; a good way to expand ownership and relationships. Shortsightedness is often a barrier to accomplishment, and planning the original of anything carefully eliminates costly remodeling. Lack of room for more needed parking, for instance, has been the downfall of some businesses with mighty potential.

Additional capacity welcomes growth, and if there is a place for the new, new will come to fill it. Build the barn bigger than today's occupancy and you'll have more control of tomorrow.

How should a boss behave?

Now that I move in big business circles with the big companies, the single most frequent comment or compliment I get is that I still work hard—longer, tougher hours than the thousands of people who work for me. "Why should you, when you don't have to?" I'm often asked. Well, back to the barnyard for the answer. It doesn't take long in and around the barn to find out who's doing the work and how much. It was a code of honor with us to keep up with or pass the top producers, not to see how little you could get away with doing. Even at the age of thirteen, when I figured I was about as much of a man as I was going to be, Dad or Grandfather could milk two cows to my one, harness two horses to my one, put on three bolts or three tires to my two, or pitch two rows of hay to my one. Whenever I'd express my frustration at not being able to outwork them they'd always say, "As long as we're the bosses and paid the most, we ought to do the most."

That made sense to me. "The Boss" was in a position to do more, be an example. The boss always took the heavy end and the toughest side and worked whether sick or well, always fed others before he ate. He was there first and left last; he was in charge and if he was a real boss he took charge by doing more than his hired people.

The boss is the leader, and he does have the privilege of assigning jobs and duties, and that's best done not by giving or shouting orders, but showing how it's done yourself, barnyard style. Too many bosses have become nothing but "trackers," forgetting that the best way to teach and inspire is by exhibiting results yourself. As Dad always said, a good way to render someone useless is to give him or her a promotion, a clipboard, and a new pickup all at the same time. "I'm paid too much to do any real work" is the up and coming curse of our country, permission to grow a big belly, drive a big car, and draw a big pension and bonus. The idea of love and respect from your crew is lost somewhere.

A farm philosophy

My management philosophy, which I learned watching Mother run a big household and gardens with limited resources, and watching Dad and my grandparents run huge farms with many crops and hundreds of livestock:

1. Trust people.

2. Work hard.
3. Never get behind.
4. Keep your word.
5. Be generous (more than fair) with neighbors, merchants, and helpers.
6. Be in control of what you have control over.
7. Give your people plenty of rope and expect them to be accountable for themselves.

Bum lambs are worth it

The Basque sheepherders who traveled Idaho when I was growing up brought their herds from the south, following the season as the grass greened, heading for the mountains. The flocks ate their way past our ranch in about four or five days, and left a trail peppered with sheep manure behind them. Tiny orphan lambs were often behind, too, to die or to nourish the coyotes. These lost or disowned little critters were called "bum lambs," because if they couldn't bum a home or a bottle they'd perish.

When found they were a child's joy and a parent's woe. What would you do if your children appeared at the door, each with a soft, cuddly, helpless baby lamb in their arms? With excitement and compassion beyond words in their face, they'd present the lamb to you for the big decision: Could they keep it or not? Even the roughest, toughest old ranch hand (all too aware of the cost and inconvenience of keeping a lamb under such conditions) couldn't pronounce the harsh sentence of "go put it out of its misery." Even they felt sorry for the kid, and so Mother was a pushover and we were in heaven.

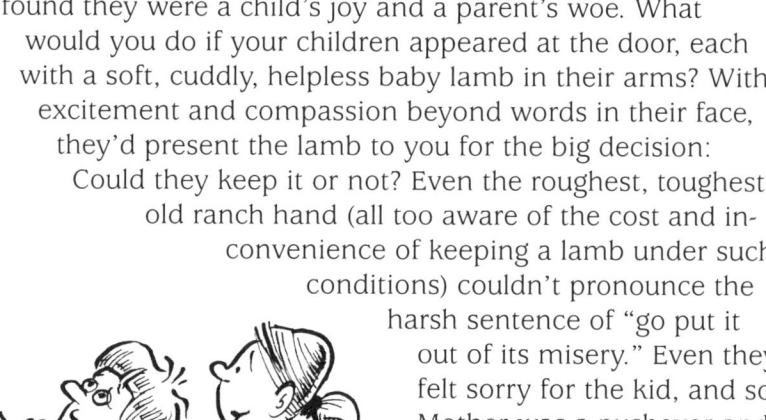

Little nipples were slipped over the top of a pop bottle of warm cow's milk, and the minute that two-days-without-food youngster found that nipple its little tail twitched in a rhythm no big band could match. It would wag a lively thank-you and then lunge vigorously at the bottle, a totally delightful sight to see. You would never care for a more appreciative animal—they adopted you as their mother, and they were so soft, woolly, and charming—it was probably one of the richest experiences a child could have.

The bum lambs were finally weaned off the bottle and went off to pasture and we gradually had less and less contact with them. We did realize they were destined to be mutton… someday. But our parents always took ours to the sale and got another to butcher, because even the old hands would have a hard time eating Mary's little lamb.

Years later, when I was grown and married, I found that my wife, though she was a town girl, had wandered out into the desert with her friends and found a bum lamb and it greatly enriched their lives as it did ours.

Life and its herd of strong, fit survivors, too, through oversight, bad timing, bad luck, or other misfortunes, leaves some bum lambs behind. People who aren't quite as swift or strong as most and have no one to turn to. Young or old or in between, they're good people who will fall by the wayside or perish if they're left out in the desert of free enterprise.

Good logical business arithmetic says leave them alone, they'll never pay for themselves. They're klutzes or duds and a drain financially. Let's just choose and keep the best people and let the rest go. That might be good for business, but it isn't right for business. Besides filling our own needs, we need to protect and help the needy. It isn't any kind of law; it's an opportunity and responsibility that comes with owning and running a business.

Over the years, influenced no doubt by my bum lamb days, I've taken in more than a few "bum" boys and girls and hand fed them and paid dearly for their stumbling. Looking back on their lives now, and on the changes I managed to make in them, it's been worth every dollar. We have a human as well as a business obligation to help and nurture those who are struggling to be fit and to work. When we take them in and nurse them along, we build not only society but ourselves. When we leave them behind to sink into the slough of the streets or welfare, it's not good for anyone concerned.

Having and practicing decency, giving some help, always blesses the helper more than the helped. By the time our "bum lambs" can

stand on their own in the pasture, they've given us some good solid schooling in charity. We all have the obligation to carry and help some disadvantaged person for a while, whether it's someone actually handicapped or just a late bloomer. I know sometimes we feel like the parent looking down on the anxious lamb-holding kids—we just don't want the emotional or financial expense. But the barnyard taught me above all that there are some long-range rewards in all our lives. And there is wisdom in doing business from the heart as well as the head. I wonder how many times in the course of your growing up *you* were a bum lamb to some relative, client, boss, friend, or business? I bet it would surprise you.

And my last and most cherished lesson from the barnyard...

Freedom is everything!

Once bred, cows take nine months, often till cold February, to deliver a calf weighing a wobbly 80-100 pounds. Since the mother was generally a milker we usually separated them after two days—the baby calf went into a tiny pen where the mother could see, lick, and moo to it, and we milked the cow (sometimes two big full bucketfuls) and fed the calf a couple of quarts of it while it was still warm.

Calves grow surprisingly fast and not even a fuzzy puppy is cuter than a baby calf. They were strong and energetic, but any big or fast moves were ended quickly by the walls of that little pen. We all grew fond of the calves and couldn't wait for the big day, the super bowl of the baby bossies, the day we turned the calves out to pasture. This was never done as it could be, with Dad or me simply opening the gate of the pen. This moment of unequalled glory was too good for that. It was announced at breakfast: "Today is calf day," and we shivered in anticipation of the show to come. After supper and chores, the whole family came out to watch as the calves went out the gate of those tiny calf cells into forty acres of green May grass.

A calf would step gingerly out of the only home it had known up till then, and conditioned by now to only move a few feet in any direction, it moved carefully, as if imagining the fence was still there. Then it ran three steps and nothing happened... ran four and then skidded to a halt. No wall yet? It raised its head and an expression of "Hey, could this be freedom?" came over its face. Sensing the release of bondage now, he made his big play—ran, made a few jumps, and then the old brakes went back in action, but still no walls. And then it sank in—he was free! His neck arched, his tail went up, and a more exquisite ballet than has ever appeared on any stage followed. The calf leaped and spun, jumped and kicked, and did the 100-yard dash so fast his feet ran out from under him. And as he skidded splendiferously there was no way appreciation for freedom could be better displayed.

It gave a tingle to all the onlookers, and it reminded me how great it is to live here in a country where we're free to do business. A grand privilege! (And a word of thanks to all those calves who convinced me that freedom is everything.)

Have any good barnyard or farm stories?

Share them with me so I can consider including them in the next edition:

Don Aslett
PO Box 700
Pocatello, ID 83204

Appendix
Teacher's Guide

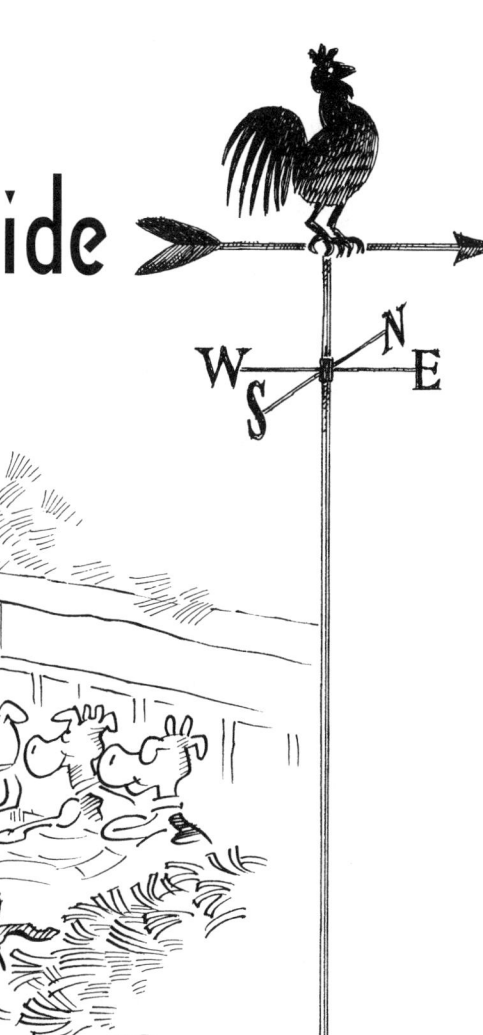

INDEX to BUSINESS SUBJECTS

General topics with page numbers.

Employee relations/management

Helping at the wrong time weakens and kills, 7
Make them scratch, 7
How to keep 'em laying, 7
Pedigree is no guarantee, 15
You feed your cows first, 18
A dull knife is worse than no knife at all, 20
Lead ropes and leadership, 21
When you get stuck, you dig yourself out, 25
All "us" animals have feelings, 27
A pat on the head saves a lot of spooking, 27
Force fails, 33
Standing asleep, 35
Animals in heat do dumb things, 35
Big udders generate poor judgment, 37
Greedy, pushy animals, 39
If you feed the stock, they stay in the corral, 55
Keep the path clear, 56
The electric fence, 58
All soils aren't the same!, 65
If they know home, they won't leave home, 68
Know where your pitchforks are!, 69
Spurs make a good horse buck, 81
No whips allowed, 81
Don't lie to your stock, 82
"Hired hands" don't solve everything, 85
The difference between pushy and pleasant, 87
Feed them right or they'll eat you up, 88
Learn and use names, 97
Surrendering the keys, 98
Middlemen, 99
Stay clear of tight situations, 102
"It's not my job…," 103
Don't spread it too thick!, 109
When you overfeed, you waste, 111
Green hay can get hot, 116
Teamwork!, 120
Cows can get fat on grass, 122
"Don't let 'em lie down…," 126
The toughest discipline, 126
Never take new gates for granted, 127
If you don't tie in your bales, your stack will fall over, 135
Dumb animals? Don't you believe it!, 136
Culling is continual, 138
Build your team before you need it, 139
Don't give up your stallions because they have a "mean streak," 142
It isn't the breed, it's the individual, 144
When the water freezes, you have to carry it, 150
How should a boss behave?, 159
A farm philosophy, 159
Bum lambs are worth it, 160

Managing the managers

Good men go to sleep in soft seats, 20
Force fails, 33

Animals in heat do dumb things, 35
Not all bulls breed, 37
Greedy, pushy animals, 39
The posts, 57
Professor barn cat, 61
All soils aren't the same!, 65
If they know home, they won't leave home, 68
Know where your pitchforks are!, 69
Don't lie to your stock, 82
Too much green stuff ruins anyone, 83
"Hired hands" don't solve everything, 85
The difference between pushy and pleasant, 87
Feed them right or they'll eat you up, 88
Surrendering the keys, 98
"It's not my job…," 103
Don't spread it too thick!, 109
When you overfeed, you waste, 111
Teamwork!, 120
Cows can get fat on grass, 122
"Don't let 'em lie down…," 126
The toughest discipline, 126
Never take new gates for granted, 127
If you can see all the wheels, you know what's going on, 134
If you don't tie in your bales, your stack will fall over, 135
Culling is continual, 138
Build your team before you need it, 139
Don't give up your stallions because they have a "mean streak," 142
When the water freezes, you have to carry it, 150
How should a boss behave?, 159
A farm philosophy, 159

Positioning yourself for business success

First roosters and second roosters, 9
Roost high, 11
Save all surprises for birthday parties!, 12
Good men go to sleep in soft seats, 20
Down wind is a bad place to be, 38
Don't park under the rafters, 39
"Root, hog, or die!," 69
Don't park in the middle of a moving herd, 74
Some hangouts that don't help, 79
The difference between pushy and pleasant, 87
Learn and use names, 97
Stay clear of tight situations, 102
Who can hurt you most, 103
Watch who you follow, 105
You swing more weight standing, 129
Ganging up, 144
There's always a crowd in the shade, 149

Attitude for success

Chest beating is only noise, 8
Another rule of the ranch, 19
The secret of early and late, 23
When you get stuck, you dig yourself out, 25
Leave things that are none of your business ALONE!, 30
Facing the chores, 40
Choice, not chance!, 54
Professor barn cat, 61
Don't stop walking just because you're wounded, 72
If you work in the herd, you're going to get stepped on!, 75
"It's not my job…," 103

Buckers get sold, 114
Stubbornness just gets you clobbered, 114
It's not "how many" flies that matters, 119
Going without makes good folks, 131
It isn't the breed, it's the individual, 144
Tie it down, 153
A crop failure isn't a farm failure, 157
Bum lambs are worth it, 160
Freedom is everything!, 162

Increasing productivity

A dull knife is worse than no knife at all, 20
The secret of early and late, 23
By hand?, 32
No cool place to work, 48
Milking manners, 51
Steers try, 54
Spud secrets, 70
Going broke on breaks, 71
Some hangouts that don't help, 79
Waiting time, 89
Too much time waving, 92
If you don't switch pastures, you'll ruin the grass, 96
The barnyard champion team, 96
The more mane, the more burrs, 100
Rake hay while the moon shines, 107
Move fast, and you won't get stung, 121
The day of rest, 141

Customer care/relations

You feed your cows first, 18
Even nice cows will kick!, 51
Fix it before it fails, 56
All soils aren't the same!, 65
Slipknots choke, 97
Learn and use names, 97
"Don't let 'em lie down…," 126

Ethics

100 trusts are lost on one bad trade, 17
Out behind the barn is in full view, 23
Leaning is losing, 124

Business management

Don't put all your eggs in one basket, 10
With assets one mistake is too many, 10
It only takes smart dogs once, 13
Timing, 25
A manure manual, 28
Weeds pull easier when small, 40
Never wait until you're out to replenish, 42
"Too many irons in the fire," 45
If you keep your head in the job, you'll seldom get kicked, 51
If it blows off the clothesline, it isn't going to stay under it, 53
Choice, not chance!, 54
Don't start the roundup until the pen is ready, 56
Fence sense, 57
Riding fence, 60
Bigger isn't necessarily better, 64
All soils aren't the same, 65
Straighten your rows at the first sign of sag, 66
There's no easy relief in a runaway, 66
If you're on your back long enough, you'll drown, 74
Go with your gut reactions, 77
But is there a "better" way?, 77
Late costs, 78

Rock picking, 84
You can't hide trouble, 88
The blue-ribbon best of all business, management, and even life lessons, 89
If your soil is shallow, supplement it!, 94
The barnyard champion team, 96
Middlemen, 99
"Predictability"—a skill you've got to have, 101
Bad smells don't always mean bad outcomes, 104
Get rid of rats, 108
The curse of the corral, the exception, 116
You can't horse around with authority 118
It's not "how many" flies that matters, 119
Leaning is losing, 124
Control by feel, 128
The reality of risk, 130
Barnyard consultants, 132
If you don't tie in your bales, your stack will fall over, 135
Culling is continual, 138
Build your team before you need it, 139
A bad year doesn't necessarily mean a bad idea, 139
New growth needs new ground, 148
Too big, too bad, 151
Do you kill the gophers… or later the stock with a broken leg?, 153
Read before you feed!, 154
Horns look bad, but it's the hooves you have to watch, 156
The experts, 155
Horns look bad, but it's the hooves you have to watch, 156
A crop failure isn't a farm failure, 157
A farm philosophy, 159

Managing facilities and equipment

You'll eventually answer for anything (junk!) you leave lying around, 14
A well-painted barn earns praise, 41
If you don't know what the weather is going to be, overdress, 44
Borrowing costs, 52
Don't start the roundup until the pen is ready, 56
Fix it BEFORE it fails, 56
Take it down before it falls down, 76
Keep your harness out of the rain, 93
Don't stockpile trouble 112
What's the #1 success word of business?, 146
Build bigger than you need right now, 158

Contracts/finance/ business dealings

It's not the cost of the chicken, it's the cost of the feed, 8
Use thick gloves when you handle barbed wire, 11
New is nice but…, 31
Know where you are!, 45
Borrowing costs, 52
That big difference between gross and net, 61
All soils aren't the same!, 65
Hardware disease, 86
Slipknots choke!, 97
Empty corrals still cost, 106
Sell the steak, not the sizzle, 110
A person's word eliminates a lot of paper, 115
Cash is more comfortable than credit, 117
"Don't let 'em lie down…," 126
The reality of risk, 130
Foul language doesn't work, 147
Tie it down, 153

What is this essay about and what does it teach?

PAGE
6   Lessons from the chickens
7   #1: Helping at the wrong time weakens and kills
   - *Managing employees:* Allowing employees to make their own way is often good and encourages growth.
7   #2: Make them scratch
   - *Managing employees:* Making things too easy for employees is not necessarily a plus.
7   #3: How to keep 'em laying
   - *Managing employees:* Give your employees the resources and support to do the job.
8   #4: It's not the cost of the chicken, it's the cost of the feed
   - *Finance:* Small costs (purchases) can require greater costs down the road.
8   #5: Chest beating is only noise
   - *Attitude:* Cockiness and intimidation of others are fast tracks for derailing a career.
9   #6: First roosters and second roosters
   - *Attitude:* Don't be afraid to be in the lead. The benefits outweigh the pressure.
10 #7 Don't put all your eggs in one basket
   - *Business management:* Learning new skills is one of the best ways to put yourself in a more secure position.
10 #8: With assets one mistake is too many
   - *Business management:* Maintain tight control of your best assets.
11 #9: Roost high!
   - *Positioning:* Cover your behind by keeping up out of the fray.
11 Use thick gloves when you handle barbed wire
   - *Contracts:* Protect yourself by staying alert for potentially dangerous situations.
12 Save all surprises for birthday parties!
   - *Positioning:* Tell bosses important information (good or bad) right away. Don't surprise them down the road.
13 It only takes smart dogs once
   - *Business management:* Admit mistakes, learn from them, and don't make the same ones again.
14 You'll eventually answer for anything (junk!) you leave lying around
   - *Managing facilities:* Stay organized and clutter-free. Get rid of things you don't need.

PAGE
15 Pedigree is no guarantee
- *Managing employees:* Don't use degrees, certifications, or portfolios alone to judge or predict an employee's ability to contribute.

17 100 trusts are lost on one bad trade
- *Business ethics:* Don't risk a lifetime of trust and solid relationships by making one questionable or dishonest move.

18 You feed your cows first
- *Customer service:* Your customers' and employees' needs should always come before your own.

19 Another rule of the ranch
- *Attitude:* Be resourceful, get maximum leverage and value by using your own creativity.

20 Good men go to sleep in soft seats
- *Positioning/Managing employees:* The soft, "cushy" route is no advantage to you or anyone else in business.

20 A dull knife is worse than no knife at all
- *Productivity/Managing employees:* Dull knives and dull employees just wear out your pocket!

21 Lead ropes and leadership
- *Leadership:* Guide employees firmly yet gently; lead them rather than give them orders.

23 The secret of early and late
- *Productivity/Attitude:* Have the discipline to be early, work hard, and stay late, if necessary.

23 Out behind the barn is in full view
- *Ethics:* Make all your actions in plain sight, or as if they were in plain sight for others to see.

25 Timing
- *Business management:* Being "early" has many advantages.

25 When you get stuck, you dig yourself out
- *Managing employees/Attitude:* Letting people work themselves out of their own problems is often the wisest approach.

27 All us animals have feelings
- *Managing employees:* Stay sensitive to those who work for you; respect them and their feelings.

27 A pat on the head saves a lot of spooking
- *Managing employees:* A little bit of encouragement can go a long way.

28 A manure manual
- *Business management:* Don't be taken in by bull droppings, avoid gossip and office politics, limit meetings, and squelch problems quickly.

PAGE
30 Leave things that are none of your business ALONE!
- *Attitude:* Minding your own business leaves a lot fewer messes to mend.

31 New is nice, but...
- *Finances:* Make do with what you've got; be frugal; avoid vanity purchases.

32 By hand?
- *Productivity:* You might be surprised at how much can still be done most efficiently by hand.

33 Force fails
- *Managing employees:* Gentle persuasion is always more effective than force.

35 Standing asleep
- *Managing employees/Productivity:* Keep your eyes out for those who look busy, but do little work.

35 Animals in heat do dumb things
- *Productivity:* Suggestive clothing and actions can easily derail productivity.

37 Big udders generate poor judgment
- *Managing employees:* The flashiest and best-looking are not necessarily the best.

37 Not all bulls breed
- *Managing the managers:* Get rid of those who don't produce.

38 Down wind is a bad place to be
- *Positioning:* Don't be afraid to be in front, take the lead, don't be left behind.

39 Don't park under the rafters
- *Positioning:* Where you situate yourself has a lot to do with what you have to put up with.

39 Greedy, pushy animals
- *Managing employees:* Don't be afraid to terminate those who won't change or improve.

40 Facing the chores
- *Attitude:* Our attitude, more than our tasks, determines our happiness.

40 Weeds pull easier when small
- *Business management:* Don't let problems fester, resolve/eliminate them early.

41 A well-painted barn earns praise
- *Managing facilities:* Keep yourself and your surroundings neat, clean, and looking good.

PAGE
42 Never wait until you're "out" to replenish
- *Business management:* Being caught "out" of anything you need—tools, supplies, or money—is just plain bad for business.

44 If you don't know what the weather is going to be, overdress
- *Positioning:* If you don't know what you need, "more" is smart.

44 Know where you are!
- *Finances:* Know exactly how much $ is going in and out.

45 "Too many irons in the fire"
- *Business management:* Having a lot to do won't overwhelm you if you're organized.

48 No cool place to work
- *Productivity:* The work still needs to be done, no matter how unfavorable the conditions are.

51 Milking manners
- *Productivity:* Keep your head in your work, and you'll get more done.

52 Borrowing costs
- *Finance/Managing equipment and facilities:* Only borrow when absolutely necessary; otherwise do without.

53 If it blows off the clothesline, it isn't going to stay under it
- *Business management:* A little extra effort and preparedness can save a lot of lost opportunity and trouble.

54 Choice, not chance!
- *Business management:* Business is not a gamble, but a series of choices—hopefully the right ones.

54 Steers try
- *Productivity:* Trying means nothing if there is no positive result.

55 If you feed the stock, they stay in the corral
- *Managing employees:* Take care of your good people, so they will stay around.

56 Don't start the roundup until the pen is ready
- *Business management/Managing facilities:* Be prepared for growth and advancement.

56 Fix it BEFORE it fails
- *Customer service/Managing equipment:* Take care of your customers—it's easier to spend a little time and resources maintaining than a lot replacing.

56 Keep the path clear
- *Managing employees:* Keep a clear vision/path for employees to follow.

PAGE
57 Fence sense
- *Business management:* Let people know where the boundaries are right at the beginning, and hold them to it. Plan those boundaries carefully, and make sure they are enforceable. Eliminate rules when they no longer apply, or are no longer needed.

58 The electric fence
- *Managing employees:* Let people know where the boundaries are, and see that they are well aware of what will happen if they violate them.

60 Riding fence
- *Business management:* Preventive maintenance saves time and headaches down the road.

61 That big difference between gross and net
- *Finance:* Don't let yourself lose sight of whether or not you are making a real profit.

61 Professor barn cat (MBA, PhD)
- *Attitude:* Like the barn cat, be quick, patient, prompt, dependable, brave, self-reliant, and grateful.

62 Bigger isn't necessarily better
- *Business management:* Bigger may mean more volume, but not necessarily more profit.

65 All soils aren't the same!
- *Managing employees/Customer service:* You can't treat everyone and everything the same.

66 Straighten your rows at the first sign of sag
- *Business management:* Nip problems in the bud—if you wait, it'll take you way off course.

66 There's no easy relief in a runaway
- *Business management:* Fix the weak spots in your business, before you have to struggle to control a large, runaway problem.

68 If they know home, they won't leave home
- *Managing employees:* Make new employees feel at home, then they're more apt to stay.

69 "Root, hog, or die!"
- *Positioning yourself for success*: Stay "hungry," and show drive and initiative.

69 Know where your pitchforks are!
- *Managing employees:* Employees are key "tools" of your business—take good care of them.

PAGE
70 Spud secrets
- *Productivity:* Being able to work long, hard, and efficiently will get you places.
71 Going broke on breaks
- *Productivity:* Meals and breaks are necessary, but keep them brief during the workday.
72 Don't stop walking just because you're wounded
- *Attitude:* Don't dodge responsibility because of a little discomfort.
74 If you're on your back long enough, you'll drown
- *Business management:* When in a pickle, don't lie there, get out ASAP.
74 Don't park in the middle of a moving herd
- *Positioning:* Wherever the action is in your business, be right in the middle of it.
75 If you work in the herd, you're going to get stepped on!
- *Attitude:* If you're in the middle of the action, expect pressure.
76 Take it down before it falls down
- *Managing facilities:* If something is falling apart or not useful anymore, get rid of it.
77 Go with your gut reactions
- *Business management:* Don't ignore your instincts; they are often more accurate than not.
77 But is there a "better" way?
- *Business management:* There is rarely one best way to do things; try something different sometimes.
78 Late costs
- *Business management:* "Later" is one of the biggest saboteurs of success in business.
79 Some hangouts that don't help
- *Productivity/Positioning:* Loafing or idleness is a danger for any business, as are the locations that encourage it.
81 Spurs make a good horse buck
- *Managing employees:* Harsh methods bring harsh reactions.
81 No whips allowed
- *Managing employees:* Prodding or forcing somebody to work harder has short-lived results.
82 Don't lie to your stock
- *Managing employees/managers:* Always keep your word, no matter how difficult it is sometimes.

PAGE
83 Too much green stuff ruins anyone
- *Managing the managers:* Too much too soon can ruin even the best of employees.

84 Rock picking
- *Business management:* Remove the little problems before they add up to big problems.

85 "Hired hands" don't solve everything
- *Managing employees/managers:* More people doesn't automatically mean more work done.

86 Hardware disease
- *Contracts:* Do your homework and know what you're getting into before you go for it.

87 The difference between pushy and pleasant
- *Managing employees:* Don't force relationships; let them develop naturally.

88 Feed them right or they'll eat you up
- *Managing employees/managers:* If you short your employees or partners, they will find ways (you won't like) to make up the difference.

88 You can't hide trouble
- *Business management:* Don't try to hide your mistakes or problems; uproot them once you discover them.

89 Waiting time
- *Productivity:* Always have another task you can work on when you are forced to interrupt your current task.

89 The blue-ribbon best of all business, management, and even life lessons
- *Business management:* Out-thinking someone is usually more effective than outrunning them.

92 Too much time waving
- *Productivity:* How to be friendly and productive at the same time.

93 Keep your harness out of the rain
- *Managing equipment:* Take good care of your tools—you will pay a high price for neglecting them.

94 If your soil is shallow, supplement it
- *Business management:* Improve what you have instead of quitting, trashing it, or moving on.

96 If you don't switch pastures, you'll ruin the grass
- *Productivity:* Switch projects every so often to keep a fresh and healthy perspective.

PAGE
96 The barnyard champion team
- *Business management/Productivity:* A strong husband and wife team can be the most powerful around.

97 Slipknots choke!
- *Customer service:* Dangerous phrases like "I'll try," "might," and "later" can really cost you.

97 Learn and use names
- *Managing employees/Customer service:* People love to hear their own names—use them!

98 Surrendering the keys
- *Managing employees:* Turning good people loose (after training) to get things done on their own is a real confidence booster.

99 Middlemen
- *Business Management/Managing employees:* Delegation isn't a sure cure for everything, nor is it free. The same is true of middlemen of any kind.

100 The more mane, the more burrs
- *Productivity:* Simplicity is a big timesaver.

101 "Predictability"—a skill you've got to have
- *Business management:* Spend time predicting and planning for the future so you can be ahead of the game.

102 Stay clear of tight situations
- *Managing employees/Positioning:* Don't get in too deep when attempting to help employees, colleagues, or fellow businesspeople.

103 "It's not my job…"
- *Attitude:* If a job needs done, be willing to tackle it or help with it, whether it was assigned to you or not.

103 Who can hurt you most
- *Positioning:* Beware of those in business who have something to push or protect.

104 Bad smells don't always mean bad outcomes
- *Business management:* Sometimes the best business deals or moves don't smell right to begin with; learn to look past the initial scent.

105 Watch who you follow…
- *Positioning:* Be careful who you follow; the one in the lead is not always the one who will lead your business to profitability.

106 Empty corrals still cost
- *Finance:* The costs of overhead mean that not even empty spaces are free.

PAGE
107 Rake hay while the moon shines
- *Productivity:* Take advantage of every opportunity to get some extra work done; don't be afraid to work late when needed.

108 Get rid of rats
- *Business management:* Keep a clean, honest working environment where dishonest people won't want to work.

109 Don't spread it too thick!
- *Managing employees:* Offer your people good incentives for working, but be careful not to overdo it.

110 Sell the steak, not the sizzle
- *Finance:* Don't get in the habit of getting paid for work not yet done.

111 When you overfeed, you waste
- *Managing employees:* Be careful not to overcompensate your people or give them too many perks; it may become the new expectation level.

112 Don't stockpile trouble
- *Managing facilities:* Dejunking costs nothing but a little time and it's one of the most profitable moves you can make.

114 Buckers get sold
- *Attitude:* Troublemakers get ousted.

114 Stubbornness just gets you clobbered
- *Attitude:* Refusing to budge or reason, even if you are right, won't do much for you in business.

115 A person's word eliminates a lot of paper
- *Contracts:* Try to do business with people for whom a handshake means as much as a signature.

116 The curse of the corral, the exception
- *Business management:* Making exceptions will eventually add up to trouble.

116 Green hay can get hot!
- *Managing employees:* Sending a green employee into an important business assignment is a bad move.

117 Cash is more comfortable than credit
- *Finance:* Be careful not to rely too much on credit; it's a good feeling and good practice to pay for things immediately and in full.

118 You can't horse around with authority
- *Business management:* Authority and respect are earned little by little.

PAGE
119 It's not "how many" flies that matters…
- *Business management:* Don't leave important documents or things lying around for people to buzz over.

120 Teamwork!
- *Managing employees/managers:* Teamwork does a lot to stave off exterior nuisances and problems.

121 Move fast, and you won't get stung
- *Productivity:* Keep moving fast; not only will you get more done, you'll feel better about doing it.

122 Cows can get fat on grass
- *Managing employees/managers:* Too much of anything can ruin people.

124 Leaning is losing
- *Ethics/Business management:* Keep your eye out for the "gradual lean," the slip in integrity, the small losses of productivity, etc. If not corrected, those gradual leans can collapse a department or business.

126 "Don't let 'em lie down…"
- *Managing employees:* Try to keep people moving and going; once they slow down or stop, it's hard to get them started again.

126 The toughest discipline
- *Managing employees:* Have the fortitude and courage to make the tough decisions when needed.

127 Never take new gates for granted
- *Managing employees:* When you are asking people to make changes, big or small, make sure you take time to explain what's in it for them (how they will benefit).

128 Control by feel
- *Business management:* Sometimes you have to go by how you feel more than what the data says. A seasoned businessperson always pays attention to his/her feelings.

129 You swing more weight standing
- *Positioning:* You think better when you are on your feet than sitting.

130 The reality of risk
- *Business management:* Be willing to take risks when necessary.

131 Going without makes good folks
- *Attitude:* Going without is very healthy sometimes; it allows you to enjoy and appreciate things more fully.

PAGE
132 Barnyard consultants
- *Business management:* Outside consultants usually have outside perspectives; you have the inside perspective… and the final responsibility.

134 If you can see all the wheels, you know what's going on
- *Business management:* Leaders should be more accountable for their actions instead of less, since their decisions are critical to a business's success.

135 If you don't tie in your bales, your stack will fall over
- *Business management:* People, goals, strategies, and plans need to be tightly interlocked in order to reach maximum potential. You can't have a lot of loose parts, no matter how good they are.

136 Dumb animals? Don't you believe it!
- *Managing employees:* All people are important and have great potential, regardless of age, national origin, or education. Treat them accordingly.

138 Culling is continual
- *Business management:* Separate the spoiled or bad apples from the bunch, or soon you'll have a bad bunch.

139 Build your team before you need it
- *Managing employees/Business management:* You have to constantly be building and developing your team, contacts, and customers, so you'll never be caught short by attrition.

139 A bad year doesn't necessarily mean a bad idea
- *Business management:* Stick with a good idea or a good plan, even if you don't see the fruits right away.

141 The day of rest
- *Productivity:* We all need a rest once in a while; take it. It will make you sharper and more productive the rest of the time.

142 Don't give up your stallions because they have a "mean streak"
- *Managing employees/managers:* Just because someone has a mean streak or is a little ornery, don't discount their talents or abilities. Look deeper. You may discover that people like these are the best of the bunch.

144 Ganging up
- *Positioning:* Stay ahead of and above the pack or you'll liable to get buried.

144 It isn't the breed, it's the individual
- *Managing employees/managers:* Don't discount someone because of their gender, age, or national origin. There are diamonds everywhere if you are looking for them.

PAGE
146 What's the #1 success word of business?
- *Managing facilities:* When you keep things clean, everything looks and feels better. It's the starting point for any successful business.

147 Foul language doesn't work
- *Business dealings:* Avoid swearing, dirty jokes, or foul language. It's never becoming or impressive.

148 New growth needs new ground
- *Business management:* You need to break new ground—do some pioneering—every so often to increase your yields.

149 There's always a crowd in the shade
- *Positioning:* Finding a sheltered area to hunker down in is not where winners are made and profits are won.

150 When the water freezes, you have to carry it
- *Managing employees/managers:* Don't let problems freeze up or ice over before you address them.

151 To big, too bad
- *Business management:* Bigger is not always better; sometimes expansion and growth can be detrimental if not handled properly.

153 Do you kill the gophers… …or later the stock with a broken leg
- *Business management:* Don't wait to deal with problems; the best time to address them is when you discover them.

153 Tie it down
- *Business dealings:* The only way to secure or assure things in business is to fully commit to them.

154 Read before you feed!
- *Business management:* Take the time to read and follow directions, and stay aware of what you are doing.

155 The experts
- *Business management:* Stick with your passions, ambitions, and goals, and you will become an expert before you realize it.

156 Horns look bad, but it's the hooves you have to watch
- *Business management:* Make sure you're worrying about… and watching… the right thing. Sometimes leaving a situation or deal is better than staying and trying to fight your way through it.

157 A crop failure isn't a farm failure
- *Business management:* Don't get yourself too worked up over small failures or disappointments; they will happen—learn from them and move on.

PAGE
158 Build bigger than you need right now
- *Managing facilities/Business management:* Always plan on and prepare for the future so you aren't always thinking in terms of the present.

159 How should a boss behave?
- *Managing employees/managers:* The best way to motivate employees to perform is to lead by example.

160 Bum lambs are worth it
- *Attitude:* Reach out and help those in need; you'll always get more in return than what you gave.

162 Freedom is everything!,
- *Attitude:* We're lucky to live in a country where we can do business freely; don't ever forget what a true blessing this is.

Alphabetical list of essays

A bad year doesn't necessarily mean a bad idea, 139
A crop failure isn't a farm failure, 157
A dull knife is worse than no knife at all, 20
A farm philosophy, 159
All soils aren't the same!, 65
All "us" animals have feelings, 27
A manure manual, 28
Animals in heat do dumb things, 35
Another rule of the ranch, 19
A pat on the head saves a lot of spooking, 27
A person's word eliminates a lot of paper, 115
A well-painted barn earns praise, 41
Bad smells don't always mean bad outcomes, 104
Barnyard consultants, 132
Bigger isn't necessarily better, 64
Big udders generate poor judgment, 37
Borrowing costs, 52
Buckers get sold, 114
Build bigger than you need right now, 158
Build your team before you need it, 139
Bum lambs are worth it, 160
But is there a "better" way?, 77
By hand?, 32
Cash is more comfortable than credit, 117
Choice, not chance!, 54
Control by feel, 128
Cows can get fat on grass, 122
Culling is continual, 138
Don't give up your stallions because they have a "mean streak", 142
"Don't let 'em lie down…", 126
Don't lie to your stock, 82
Don't park in the middle of a moving herd, 74
Don't park under the rafters, 39
Don't spread it too thick!, 109
Don't start the roundup until the pen is ready, 56
Don't stockpile trouble, 112
Don't stop walking just because you're wounded, 72
Down wind is a bad place to be, 38
Do you kill the gophers… …or later the stock with a broken leg?, 153
Dumb animals? Don't you believe it!, 136
Empty corrals still cost, 106
Facing the chores, 40
Feed them right or they'll eat you up, 88
Fence sense, 57
Fix it BEFORE it fails, 56
Force fails, 33
Foul language doesn't work, 147
Freedom is everything!, 162
Ganging up, 144
Get rid of rats, 108
Going broke on breaks, 71
Going without makes good folks, 131
Good men go to sleep in soft seats, 20
Go with your gut reactions, 77
Greedy, pushy animals, 39
Green hay can get hot!, 116
Hardware disease, 86
"Hired hands" don't solve everything, 85
Horns look bad, but it's the hooves you have to watch, 156

How should a boss behave?, 159
If it blows off the clothesline, it isn't going to stay under it, 53
If they know home, they won't leave home, 68
If you're on your back long enough, you'll drown, 74
If you can see all the wheels, you know what's going on, 134
If you don't know what the weather is going to be, overdress, 44
If you don't switch pastures, you'll ruin the grass, 96
If you don't tie in your bales, your stack will fall over, 135
If you feed the stock, they stay in the corral, 55
If your soil is shallow, supplement it!, 94
If you work in the herd, you're going to get stepped on!, 75
It's not "how many" flies that matters, 119
"It's not my job…", 103
It isn't the breed, it's the individual, 144
It only takes smart dogs once, 13
Keep the path clear, 56
Keep your harness out of the rain, 93
Know where you are!, 44
Know where your pitchforks are!, 69
Late costs, 78
Lead ropes and leadership, 21
Leaning is losing, 124
Learn and use names, 97
Leave things that are none of your business ALONE, 30
Middlemen, 99
Milking manners, 51
Move fast, and you won't get stung, 121

Never take new gates for granted, 127
Never wait until you're "out" to replenish, 42
New growth needs new ground, 148
New is nice, but…, 31
No cool place to work, 48
Not all bulls breed, 37
No whips allowed, 81
100 trusts are lost on one bad trade, 17
Out behind the barn is in full view, 23
Pedigree is no guarantee, 15
"Predictability"—a skill you've got to have, 101
Professor barn cat (MBA, PhD), 61
Rake hay while the moon shines, 107
Read before you feed!, 154
Riding fence, 60
Rock picking, 84
"Root, hog, or die!", 69
Save all surprises for birthday parties!, 12
Sell the steak, not the sizzle, 110
Slipknots choke!, 97
Some hangouts that don't help, 79
Spud secrets, 70
Spurs make a good horse buck, 81
Standing asleep, 35
Stay clear of tight situations, 102
Steers try, 54
Straighten your rows at the first sign of sag, 66
Stubbornness just gets you clobbered, 114
Surrendering the keys, 98
Take it down before it falls down, 76
Teamwork!, 120
That big difference between gross and net, 61
The barnyard champion team, 96

The blue-ribbon best of all business, management, and even life lessons, 89
The curse of the corral, the exception, 116
The day of rest, 141
The difference between pushy and pleasant, 87
The electric fence, 58
The experts, 155
The more mane, the more burrs, 100
There's always a crowd in the shade, 149
There's no easy relief in a runaway, 66
The reality of risk, 130
The secret of early and late, 23
The toughest discipline, 126
Tie it down, 153
Timing, 25
Too big, too bad, 151
"Too many irons in the fire", 45
Too much green stuff ruins anyone, 83
Too much time waving, 92
Use thick gloves when you handle barbed wire, 11
Waiting time, 89
Watch who you follow…, 105
Weeds pull easier when small, 40
What's so fascinating about a barnyard?, 5
What's the #1 success word of business?, 146
When the water freezes, you have to carry it, 150
When you get stuck, you dig yourself out, 25
When you overfeed, you waste, 111
Who can hurt you most, 103

You'll eventually answer for anything (junk!) you leave lying around, 14
You can't hide trouble, 88
You can't horse around with authority, 118
You feed your cows first, 18
You swing more weight standing, 129

Other Aslett books you won't want to miss...

How I Swept My Way to the Top: The Don Aslett Story
576 pages, 300+ photos

The subtitle of my autobiography is "Taking a common job to uncommon success." You could also call it, "Everything you ever wanted to know about Don A., and more." In more than 500 pages (full of pictures, pictures, pictures!) there are answers to just about every one of the questions people have asked me over the years.

- A look at the young Don Aslett, growing up on the ranch and farm in the West. My school and college years, everything from my skirmishes and lessons on the playground to discovery of the opposite sex.
- My early mission and young married days, and the building of my cleaning empire; along with the struggles, nutty and hilarious happenings, and learning experiences along the way.
- My brave first step into authorship, and the wild ride that followed, including many behind-the-scenes stories of my adventures in publishing, public relations, and publicity.

The book will bring you right up to the present, too, with my latest ideas and undertakings, my master plan, and even some of the philosophies that helped me to accomplish it all.

"A must-read book for anyone who aspires to form and grow a business in America. Don clearly describes the steps he took in building his company, from childhood through university education to founding and operating a nationwide company. It is especially interesting to read how he integrated his personal life with his professional activities.

"Many young people growing up in today's world believe that the government owes them an easy and successful life. It would even appear that many believe socialism would be an ideal form of government. Don's book shows that a person's hard work in our free society can lead to a successful company and a happy life."

—JACK I. HOPE, ENTREPRENEUR AND PROMINENT AVIATION ENGINE DESIGNER (AND FARMER), HILLSBORO, OH

"We at Janiczek & Co. have attended just about every time management seminar in existence and read just about every time management book on the market in search of how we and our clients can be more productive. After years of finding some pretty good aids, we have finally found THE BOOK—the very best, in our opinion, on productivity…"

—JANICZEK & COMPANY, LTD.
PROFESSIONAL FINANCIAL ADVISORS

Done! How to accomplish twice as much in half the time
207 pages, illustrated

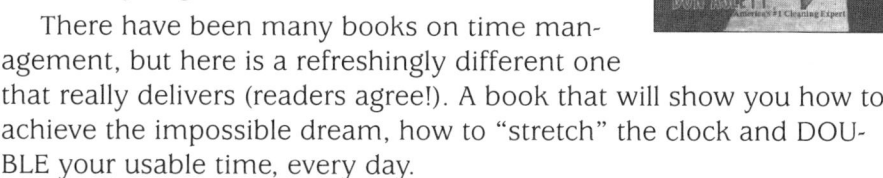

The man who helps Americans do their housework 75% faster and better now shows how you can apply this magic to every area of your life. This is the book Don wrote to answer the thousands of people who have asked him, "How do you get so much done, Don?"

There have been many books on time management, but here is a refreshingly different one that really delivers (readers agree!). A book that will show you how to achieve the impossible dream, how to "stretch" the clock and DOUBLE your usable time, every day.

"***Done!*** *is an entertaining, common sense page-turner of a book on productivity by a very productive person. It is not a compilation of research written in a stuffy, academic way, nor is it a hook to buy an elaborate and expensive calendar or software. It is, quite simply a highly-readable, powerfully motivating book you'll find difficult to put down.*"

- How to double or triple what you can do (and only feel more energetic afterward)
- How to overcome that big stumbling block of getting started
- The #1 secret for keeping yourself on track
- The right way to approach lists, schedules, and priorities
- How to boost not just your efficiency, but your effectiveness
- How to pitch time-stealing mental and physical junk
- How to multiply the highs of accomplishment, and much more!

CLEANING – New Editions!

HELP! Around the House
NEW Book!

Is There Life After Housework?
2nd Edition

Pet Clean-Up Made Easy
2nd Edition

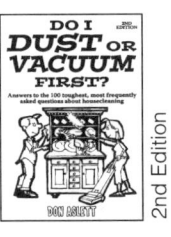
Do I Dust or Vacuum First?
2nd Edition

Make Your House Do the Housework

Don Aslett's Stain Buster's Bible

The Guide to Hard Wood Floor Care & Maintenance

Don Aslett – No Time to Clean!

Don Aslett's Clean in a Minute

The Cleaning Encyclopedia

Who Says It's a Woman's Job to Clean?

DECLUTTERING

Weekend Makeover
2nd Edition*

Clutter's Last Stand
2nd Edition

The Office Clutter Cure
2nd Edition

Don Aslett's Clutter Free! Finally & Forever

For Packrats Only

AUDIO CD

Dejunk Live!

* Formerly *Lose 200 Lbs. This Weekend*

VIDEOS

Don Aslett's Video Seminar – Is There Life After Housework?

Clean in a Minute

Restroom Maintenance & Sanitation VIDEO

PROFESSIONAL CLEANERS

Cleaning up for a Living

The Professional Cleaner's Personal Handbook

How to Upgrade and Motivate Your Cleaning Crews

Construction Cleanup

CLIP ART CD

Don Aslett's Professional Cleaner's Clip Art

Painting without Fainting

WRITING

Get Organized, Get Published! 225 Ways to Make Time for Success

How to Write & Sell Your First Book

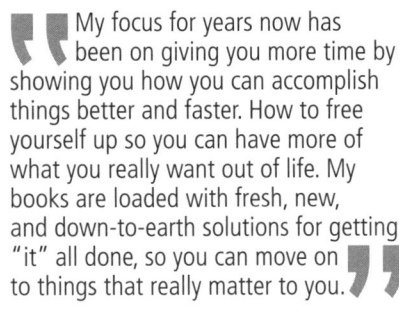

"My focus for years now has been on giving you more time by showing you how you can accomplish things better and faster. How to free yourself up so you can have more of what you really want out of life. My books are loaded with fresh, new, and down-to-earth solutions for getting "it" all done, so you can move on to things that really matter to you."

NEW AUTOBIOGRAPHY!

BUSINESS, MANAGEMENT

2nd Edition** | 2nd Edition

** Formerly *How to Have a 48-Hour Day*

MAIL your order to:
Don Aslett
PO Box 700
Pocatello ID 83204
CALL: 888-748-3535
          208-232-3535
FAX: 208-235-5481
ONLINE: www.Aslett.com

☐ Don, please put my name and the enclosed list of my friends on your mailing list for the **Clean Report** bulletin and catalog.

TITLE	Retail	Qty	Amt
Barnyard to Boardroom: Business Basics	$14.99		
Clean in a Minute	$6.95		
DVD Clean in a Minute	$14.99		
Cleaning Up for a Living	$39.95		
Clutter Free! Finally & Forever	$12.99		
Clutter's Last Stand, 2nd Edition	$9.95		
Construction Cleanup	$19.95		
Dejunk LIVE! Audio CD	$14.99		
Don Aslett's Stainbuster's Bible	$13.95		
Done! (Formerly **How to Have a 48-Hour Day**)	$9.95		
Do I Dust Or Vacuum First? 2nd Edition	$9.95		
For Packrats Only	$13.95		
Get Organized, Get Published	$18.99		
HELP! Around the House *NEW!*	$9.95		
How I Swept My Way to the Top	$24.99		
How to Be #1 With Your Boss	$9.99		
How to Handle 1,000 Things at Once	$12.99		
How to Upgrade & Motivate Your Cleaning Crew	$19.95		
How to Write & Sell Your First Book	$14.95		
Is There Life After Housework? 2nd Edition	$9.95		
DVD/VHS Is There Life After Housework?	$19.95		
Make Your House Do the Housework	$19.95		
No Time To Clean!	$12.95		
Painting Without Fainting	$9.99		
Pet Clean-Up Made Easy, 2nd Edition	$9.95		
Professional Cleaner's Clip Art CD	$29.95		
DVD/VHS Restroom Sanitation (with Quiz Booklet)	$69.95		
Speak Up	$12.99		
The Cleaning Encyclopedia	$16.95		
The Office Clutter Cure, 2nd Edition	$9.95		
The Professional Cleaner's Handbook	$19.95		
Weekend Makeover (Formerly Lose 200 Lbs...)	$9.95		
Who Says It's A Woman's Job to Clean?	$5.95		
Wood Floor Care	$9.95		

Shipping: $3.25 for first book or video plus 75¢ for each additional.	Subtotal	
	Idaho residents only add 5% Sales Tax	
	Shipping	
	TOTAL	

☐ Check enclosed ☐ Visa ☐ MasterCard ☐ Discover ☐ American Express

Card No. _____

Exp Date _____ Phone _____

Signature X _____
Ship to:
Your Name _____

Street Address _____

City ST Zip _____

CLEANING – New Editions!

DECLUTTERING

 AUDIO CD

* Formerly *Lose 200 Lbs. This Weekend*

VIDEOS

PROFESSIONAL CLEANERS

CLIP ART CD

WRITING

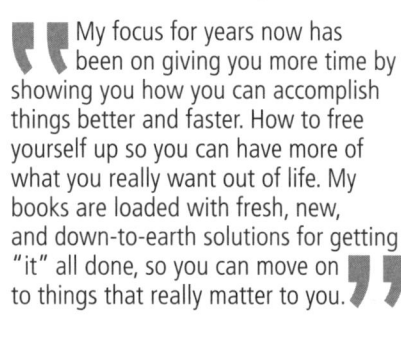

" My focus for years now has been on giving you more time by showing you how you can accomplish things better and faster. How to free yourself up so you can have more of what you really want out of life. My books are loaded with fresh, new, and down-to-earth solutions for getting "it" all done, so you can move on to things that really matter to you. "

NEW AUTOBIOGRAPHY!

BUSINESS, MANAGEMENT

2nd Edition**

2nd Edition

** Formerly *How to Have a 48-Hour Day*

MAIL your order to:
Don Aslett
PO Box 700
Pocatello ID 83204
CALL: 888-748-3535
     208-232-3535
FAX: 208-235-5481
ONLINE: www.Aslett.com

☐ Don, please put my name and the enclosed list of my friends on your mailing list for the **Clean Report** bulletin and catalog.

Barn 2008

TITLE	Retail	Qty	Amt
Barnyard to Boardroom: Business Basics	$14.99		
Clean in a Minute	$6.95		
DVD Clean in a Minute	$14.99		
Cleaning Up for a Living	$39.95		
Clutter Free! Finally & Forever	$12.99		
Clutter's Last Stand, 2nd Edition	$9.95		
Construction Cleanup	$19.95		
Dejunk LIVE! Audio CD	$14.99		
Don Aslett's Stainbuster's Bible	$13.95		
Done! (Formerly **How to Have a 48-Hour Day**)	$9.95		
Do I Dust Or Vacuum First? 2nd Edition	$9.95		
For Packrats Only	$13.95		
Get Organized, Get Published	$18.99		
HELP! Around the House *NEW!*	$9.95		
How I Swept My Way to the Top	$24.99		
How to Be #1 With Your Boss	$9.99		
How to Handle 1,000 Things at Once	$12.99		
How to Upgrade & Motivate Your Cleaning Crew	$19.95		
How to Write & Sell Your First Book	$14.95		
Is There Life After Housework? 2nd Edition	$9.95		
DVD/VHS Is There Life After Housework?	$19.95		
Make Your House Do the Housework	$19.95		
No Time To Clean!	$12.99		
Painting Without Fainting	$9.99		
Pet Clean-Up Made Easy, 2nd Edition	$9.95		
Professional Cleaner's Clip Art CD	$29.95		
DVD/VHS Restroom Sanitation (with Quiz Booklet)	$69.95		
Speak Up	$12.99		
The Cleaning Encyclopedia	$16.95		
The Office Clutter Cure, 2nd Edition	$9.95		
The Professional Cleaner's Handbook	$19.95		
Weekend Makeover (Formerly Lose 200 Lbs…)	$9.95		
Who Says It's A Woman's Job to Clean?	$5.95		
Wood Floor Care	$9.95		

Shipping:
$3.25 for first book or video plus 75¢ for each additional.

Subtotal	
Idaho residents only add 5% Sales Tax	
Shipping	
TOTAL	

☐ Check enclosed ☐ Visa ☐ MasterCard ☐ Discover ☐ American Express

Card No. _____

Exp Date _____ Phone _____

Signature X _____

Ship to:
Your Name _____

Street Address _____

City ST Zip _____

Don Aslett
KEYNOTE SPEAKER

Don Aslett is:
ATTENTION GRABBING
Fresh, new!
MOTIVATIONAL
Inspiring!
INSPIRATIONAL
Uplifting!
ENTERTAINING
A laugh a minute!

After 10,000 presentations, Don is still:

- Enthused
- Experienced
- Available

For…
- Keynote speeches
- Seminars
- Workshops
- Training
- Consulting

Proven areas of expertise:

- Decluttering
- Increasing productivity
- Time management
- Business management
- Motivating staff
- Upping self-worth
- Improving work ethics
- Writing and publishing

50 years in business—learn from a man who has done it all! Rapid-fire presentation, fast-paced wit, action-packed demonstrations, new fun facts, and the ability to bring everyone to side-splitting laughter makes Don a popular presenter.

For more information and availability contact Tobi:
PO Box 700, Pocatello, ID 83204 • 208-232-3535 • tobi@aslett.com